MW01201418

Medicinal Plants of the Southern Appalachians

Patricia Kyritsi Howell

BOTANOLOGOS BOOKS

Mountain City, Georgia 2006

Note to the reader: The information in this reference is not intended to substitute for expert medical advice or treatment; it is designed to help you make informed choices. The remedies, approaches, and techniques described herein are meant to supplement, and not to be a substitute for, professional care or treatment. They should not be used to treat a serious ailment without prior consultation with a qualified health care professional. Dosage information is provided as a general guide. The opinions stated herein are not guaranteed or warranted to produce any particular results. Care has been taken to confirm the accuracy of the information presented and to describe generally accepted practices. However, the author and publisher are not responsible for errors or omissions or for any consequences from application of the information in this book and make no warranty, expressed or implied, with respect to the contents of this publication.

Henry David Thoreau quote used with permission of Dover Publications.

For permission, contact the publisher at:
BotanoLogos Books
Post Office Box W
Mountain City, Georgia 30562 USA
www.botanologos.com

Printed in the United States
10 Digit ISBN 0-9774905-0-5
13 Digit ISBN 978-0-9774905-0-9
LCCN: 2005910568

Book design: J. L. Saloff
Cover Design: Stephen Walker
Cover Photo *Passiflora incarnata*: Martin Wall

To the memory of my grandfather,
Ioannis E. Kyritsis

Table of Contents

Medicinal Plants of the Southern Appalachians

Acknowledgements

I wrote this book for my friend, Appalachian folk artist Linda Anderson. Her courage and vision as an artist, and her tenacious commitment to keep alive family traditions of living in rhythm with the earth and moon inspired me to write down all that the plants have taught me.

Many of the insights in this book spring directly from my experiences over the past 14 years with students, many of whom have become dear friends. I am especially grateful to Liz Casey, Lisa Coolidge, Patti Denike, Josiah Garrett, Ginger Kogelschatz, Leigh Lytle, Karen Maddox, Kersten Mueller, Monique Mueller, Jane Nelson, Shannon Pable, Diana Ross, John Stowe, McKenzie Wren and all my friends in the Georgia Herbalists Guild.

I am deeply grateful to Marie Carpenter, Paulette Carpenter, Ann Moore and especially Robert Murray for inviting my students and me to make ourselves at home among the rich Appalachian history of the Foxfire Center in Mountain City, Georgia.

Inspiration was provided by Donna Ball, Fran Gatins, Joe Gatins, Darlene Roth and Susan Wynn, as they pursued their own paths as writers. I am indebted to Francesca Starr for helping me find my voice. Thanks to Dale O'Brien for showing me the way on his big maps. I have also been supported by the guidance of medical anthropologist, Dooley Worth. Her brilliant insights and faith in me as a writer have been essential.

I am grateful to the skilled team that helped me complete this book: Karen Maddox, Connie Monson and Pam Winter polished off the last rough edges; Jamie Saloff translated my words into visual art; Martin Wall generously shared his radiant passionflower photograph; Stephen Walker created the beautiful cover. I am also indebted to Karen Bentley and Sarah Kyle, whose elegant gifts of language helped to clarify my ideas. Thanks to Sharon Ennis for asking the right questions.

My family and friends believed in me, and have steadily provided love and support: Brett Baker, Jennafer Baker, David and Mary Ann Butler, Patti Dobrowolski, Rosalie and Ira Dornstein, Maria Hatziyianni, Peter Randlette, Lee Shaver, Anna Stephanaki, Ioannis Stephanakis, Margarita Stephanaki, Pam Winter and all my cousins. Special thanks to my mother, Betty, and my sisters, Sharon Hickey and Kathi Hildebrandt.

It was the enthusiasm, considerable skills as a writer and editor, unceasing love, and encouragement of Robinette Kennedy that nurtured the seed of possibility that resulted in this book. Her visionary wisdom has transformed my work, and my life.

Introduction

I grew up on the tall grass prairies of northern Illinois and was well into my thirties the first time I walked into a deciduous cove forest in the southern Appalachian Mountains. I remember sitting along a path crowded by many of the medicinal plants I used often in my work with herbs. The hillside above me was covered with black and blue cohosh, partridgeberry, Solomon's seal, and maidenhair fern. Plants I had only known as dried leaves and roots in carefully labeled jars were suddenly gloriously alive. I felt I was among friends.

A few years later, I moved to the southern Appalachians. Now, growth cycles of the native medicinal herbs around my house on the edge of a great wild forest have become my markers for the passing seasons. When my sister calls to tell me she is coming south for a visit, I think: *When the lady's-slipper blooms, she will be here.* And when the first goldenrod blossom appears in late summer, I know it's time to begin making preparations for winter.

This seasonal cadence is ancient. The Appalachians are the oldest mountains on earth, formed more than 200 million years ago by shifting tectonic plates that eroded into undulating ridges interspersed with a multitude of deeply forested coves. The cove forest is a unique ecological sanctuary, blessed with rich soil and abundant rain that shelters one of the world's most botanically diverse temperate rainforests.

The region known as the southern Appalachians begins in the New River Valley in southwestern Virginia. It extends south through portions of the Allegheny Mountains, then into the

Cumberland Plateau, Smoky Mountains, and Shenandoah Valley, encompassing the entire southern range of the Blue Ridge Mountains along with the Black Mountains.

Here, more than 3,000 species of trees, shrubs and herbaceous plants can be found. Of these, 100 genera are endemic. Sassafras, blue cohosh, ginseng, witch hazel, and many other natives of the eastern woodlands grow here and in two other places: the Ozark mountains of Arkansas and eastern Asia. This phenomenon, known as plant disjunction, is the only remaining evidence of an ancient forest that covered the Northern Hemisphere 70 million years ago. The unique mountain geography of the Ozarks, eastern Asia and the southern Appalachians appears to have harbored plants in relative isolation, allowing them to survive millennia of environmental changes in the surrounding terrain.

The medicinal uses of 45 native plants that grow within the southern Appalachian region are the focus of this book. Although all these plants are found growing within the region, their range is not limited to this area. Because three distinct plant populations overlap here, some of the book's plants may be found as far north as Nova Scotia, west to Kansas, and throughout the Southeast. For example, black cohosh and blue cohosh are found in woodlands of the northern Appalachians. Passionflower and wild yam species are also found in tropical climates from the Gulf Coast of North America into Central America. Finally, there is a diverse group of endemic southern Appalachian plants, such as yellow root.

★ Plants with Deep Roots

The history of southern Appalachian medicinal plants is at least as old as the sophisticated healing practices of the Cherokee Indians, whose knowledge of the region's flora is legendary. The Cherokee system of using local plant medicines was far more sophisticated than that of the first Europeans in North America. By the time Europeans arrived, it was common for most Cherokee people to be able to recognize and use several hundred medicinal and edible plants. Tribal healing specialists may have known the medicinal values of as many as 800 local plants.

The first Europeans in North America immediately recognized the value of the botanical wealth in Appalachian forests. Centuries of overuse had severely depleted sources of wild herbs in the European countryside, and people were eager to find new medicines. European botanists frequently journeyed through the southern Appalachians, documenting and collecting new and unusual plants, always looking for new medicines.

The bark and roots of the sassafras tree were one of the first North American medicinal plants to be introduced to Europe. As early as 1603, British merchants from the city of Bath organized expeditions to gather Virginia's sassafras roots and bring them back to Europe. Sassafras tea, known as "saloop," was considered a panacea capable of restoring health and vitality. It was all the rage in the tea shops of London and Paris, something like the café lattes fashion that started on the west coast of North America in the 1980s.

The sassafras craze was the beginning of 400 years of plundering southern Appalachian woodland plants. Since then, tons of ginseng, goldenseal, bethroot, bloodroot and other native plants have been collected each year. As recently as 2001, around 420,000 pounds of wild black cohosh root were harvested in western North Carolina forests alone. By 2005, that number is believed to have doubled, as demand for the herb increases. Many southern Appalachian woodland medicinal herbs are now classified as endangered or threatened throughout most of their natural range.

Native plant medicines were important to the survival of European people who settled in the Southern Appalachians. The harsh mountain terrain made travel difficult. Largely because they had no other choice, people in isolated communities relied heavily upon local medicinal plants for most of their health care needs. Their traditional methods of healing incorporated many native plants along with the more familiar herbs from European folk medicine, such as peppermint, horehound, and comfrey. Their mastery of an eclectic assortment of remedies is evident by their survival, and it is possible that many of us would not be alive today were it not for their knowledge of herbal medicine.

In Anthony Cavender's study of folk medicine in southern Appalachia, he found that many people living in rural communities were using herbal folk remedies to treat health problems as recently as the years immediately following World War II. Many well-known folk healers throughout the region had thriving practices using herbal remedies. Stories recorded in the *Foxfire* books indicate that throughout most of the twentieth century it was common for people born and reared in the mountains of north Georgia and western North Carolina to have some knowledge of how to use local medicinal plants.

One of these people is my 94-year-old neighbor, Maude. Her family settled in northeast Georgia seven generations ago. Maude still lives in the house where she was born, keeps chickens, and grows and cans most of her family's food. Whenever she has a cold, Maude makes up a strong tea of local plants she gathers near her home. She tells me that the bitter tea, mixed with a liberal amount of honey from her husband's bees, has never let her down. Even her grown children still ask her to brew it for them when they are sick. Maude doesn't remember the names of all the plants she collects, but she does remember that when she was a child she helped her mother and grandmother collect the same plants. She says that these herbs work better than anything she's been given by a doctor. However, Maude also reports that no one in her family is interested in learning about the plants, and she feels certain that this information will die with her. Within one generation, as access to pharmaceutical drugs has increased, the use of native plant medicines has become a quaint reminder of times gone by, similar to churning butter or dipping candles by hand.

★ The Illusion of Abundance

Like many former hippies, I grew up with a vision of living simply on the earth. I still take that vision seriously, although I recognize that I live in a culture based upon the delusion that we will continue to have access to an unlimited supply of petroleum. This mass delusion fuels the flame of globalization and our government's willingness to do anything for petroleum: wage illegal and immoral wars, destroy the environment, fail to provide basic necessities to our citizens, and worse. At our present rate of consumption, the earth's supply of petroleum will peak around 2008. After that, in ways that are probably impossible for most of us to imagine, energy experts predict we will abruptly learn to value local resources as we adjust to life without the luxury of products trucked or flown in over great distances.

How will dwindling supplies of petroleum affect herbalism as it is practiced today, herbalism that is often based on a growing dependence on imported herbs? Sophisticated marketing has convinced many of us that rare expensive plants from South America or Siberia are more effective medicine than our local native plants. The drive to cash in on the latest fashion in herbalism is not new. It's the same force that motivated European botanists three hundred years ago to battle their way through thickets of rhododendron and dog hobble.

Like an Appalachian plant over harvested to the brink of extinction, many of today's "newly discovered" medicinal herbs from other parts of the world are also collected in ways that destroy their native habitats. While these herbs may be beneficial remedies, if they are being grown or harvested in a non-sustainable manner, then our buying them contributes to the same destructive cycle.

In light of my concerns about dwindling petroleum supplies and the impact of my herb-buying habits, I have often wondered what I would do if I were totally dependent on herbs I could gather myself. What if my local herb shop closed? What if I couldn't place a phone order for almost any herb in the world and find it delivered to my door within days?

With these questions in mind, I became a serious student of the native medicinal plants that thrive in the southern Appalachians. I have researched the written and oral history of each plant included in this book. I've used these plants in my clinical practice and taught students in my herb classes how to use them. I've discussed their uses with my herb colleagues and collected anecdotes from numerous sources. Most importantly, I have become a patient daily observer of the plants growing where I live.

Local native plants that intrigue me most are those with roots deep in the folk medicine culture of southern Appalachia, as well as those that are an essential part of the local ecology. Many medicinal plants from other parts of the world—such as dandelion, plantain, chickweed and mullein—are now so common throughout the region it's hard to believe that they, like me, are relative newcomers whom botanists refer to as naturalized.

Does it really matter whether a plant is native or naturalized? To an herbalist, both categories contain important medicines. Herb books that describe the use of most naturalized plants, traditionally used in Western, or European, herbalism are easy enough to find. This book's unique contribution to herbalism is its focus on native plants of the southern Appalachians.

★ Reclaiming an Old Path

For many years, the Centers for Disease Control have cautioned doctors and other medical professionals against the overuse of antibiotics because this practice leads to the development of untreatable bacterial infections. Each year the FDA recalls several widely used pharmaceutical drugs from the market, because their manufacturers failed to disclose certain dangerous or life-threatening side effects. In an attempt to increase sales and profits, drug companies have responded by marketing prescription drugs directly to consumers.

There is no doubt that the medical industry's questionable marketing practices affect the way health care and healing are practiced in this country. Our culture teaches us that only conventionally trained medical professionals have the authority to treat illness. Many of us have swallowed this propaganda because we do not see ourselves as responsible for our own well-being. We have no idea how to treat the simplest health problems such as a common cold or a slow healing wound. In truth, humans have been responsible for their own healing for a very long time.

While this book, at first glance, may appear to be a guide to the use of the native medicinal plants of the southern Appalachians, that is only one of its roles. This book is actually a manual for amnesia recovery, designed to revitalize your intuitive ability to use wild plants for healing. How to use these remedies is ancient knowledge, something we carry in our cellular memory whether we are conscious of it or not. The challenge: to expand your capacity for intuitive, instinctive ways of knowing until it becomes so much a part of your every day life that it feels like second nature. I can assure you that the capacity to experience a healing relationship with medicinal plants is still alive in most everyone, even people who've never known how it feels to be healed by a plant.

This book encourages you to restore your ability to use medicinal plants and make stronger political connections between personal and environmental health issues in order to move away from relying on pharmaceutical drugs—and other health-destroying practices—and towards routinely using teas, salves, tinctures and other simple home remedies that promote healing.

The path that leads to healing with plants is an old one that many have traveled before you. But it is still easy to follow, if you slow down enough to learn from the plants that grow around you.

How to Use This Book

This book explains how to use 45 medicinal plants native to the southern Appalachians. Anyone who has spent time in the area may be familiar with many of the plants in this book, as the list includes some of the region's most famous wildflowers. I have deliberately left out several well-known medicinal plants, such as goldenseal and lady's-slipper, whose wild populations teeter on the brink of extinction. Until sufficient quantities are available from cultivated sources, these fragile native plants must be allowed to regenerate themselves in peace.

For easy reference, information about each plant is sorted by common name, botanical name, description, key medicinal action, and part of the plant used as a medicine. You'll also find information about the traditional and current uses of each plant, harvesting and therapeutic guidelines.

Please note that the information provided here about harvesting wild plants is intended only for personal use. If you are using native plants for commercial enterprises, in the Resources section you will find a list of reputable sources of organically grown and ethically harvested herbs.

✦ Plant Names

The plants are organized by the common names most frequently used in the southern Appalachians. Common names are often colorful and descriptive but not always a reliable way to accurately identify specific plants. To positively identify a plant, you must know its genus and species name. These names, based on the system of plant taxonomy, provide an international language for talking about particular plants.

A plant's family and botanical names describe its particular family, genus, and species. In some cases, only one genus and species are used medicinally. For example, *Caulophyllum thalictroides*, or blue cohosh, is the only plant of that genus and species used medicinally. In other cases several or all species of a particular genus may be used. This is true in the case of the genus *Solidago* or goldenrod. With more than 30 species growing in the Appalachians, all are considered to have similar properties and have been used as medicines. When referring to goldenrod, it is common to see its botanical name written as *Solidago spp.* The abbreviation *spp.* indicates that more than one species is used.

The heading, Related Species, refers to other medicinal plants that are used similarly. Some related species are native to the Appalachians; others are naturalized; and many don't grow here at all unless they are cultivated in gardens. For example, the European species of gentian, *Gentiana lutea*, is widely used as a digestive bitter and is available commercially. The Appalachian species, *Gentiana clausa*, is used in exactly the same way, though it is not available on the herb market.

Even if botanical Latin is new to you, take the time to note the genus and species given for each plant (in italics) to be sure that you are collecting or buying the correct plant. To learn more about botanical names, plant families, etc., an excellent introduction can be found in *Botany in a Day* by Thomas Elpel. (*See* the Bibliography.)

✦ Botanical Descriptions

Scientific methods of teaching field botany ask us to switch off diffuse awareness of nature's kaleidoscope in favor of a one-pointed perspective that mentally dissects a living, breathing plant into precise botanical terms. For most of us, compartmentalizing is neither easy nor pleasurable, but often necessary when driving on freeways and navigating through life in a city where our ability to relax must be overridden in the interest of survival.

In contrast, relaxing in wild places is a sensual feast: the feeling of sun-warmed air on the skin and the soothing sounds of wind rustling through a thousand leaves painted every imaginable shade of green. Henry David Thoreau, a great observer of the natural world and one of my inspirations, described the value of allowing nature to soften his awareness:

> *I must walk more with free senses...I must let my senses wander as my thoughts, my eyes see without looking...the more you look the less you will observe...Be not preoccupied with looking. Go not to the object; let it come to you...What I need is not to look at all, but a true sauntering of the eye.*[1]

Actively enlisting the senses in getting to know plants connects our modern consciousness with an ancient, time-honored way of learning. Experiencing a plant's texture, color, taste, and aroma creates a lasting impression of its many characteristics. Allowing the senses to lead the way, we begin to perceive patterns in nature that are not revealed to us in any other way. One of the most powerful ways of "seeing" a medicinal plant is to close your eyes and touch the surface of a leaf, dig your fingers deep into the damp earth where the plant grows, feel the shape of a living root, take a leaf from the plant and chew it, and stretch out flat on the ground beside the plant to enjoy a butterfly's eye view of the plant's perspective on the world.

The botanical descriptions in this book are designed to nudge you towards this way of knowing the plants by including information for all your senses. A glossary is provided to help you decode the botanical terms used in this book.

To see colored photos of each plant included here, you are invited to use as a reference *A Guide to Medicinal Plants and Herbs of Eastern and Central North America* by Stephen Foster and James A. Duke (New York: Houghton Mifflin Company, 2000). Beneath the botanical description of each plant, I have listed the page numbers of the plant's photo and description in the Foster and Duke text, e.g., MPH: pp. 301-302.

✷ Key Actions

Western culture's herbal tradition traces its roots to classic Greek texts on botanical medicine that classified plants according to their actions. Actions describe a plant's physiological effect. Describing a plant in terms of its actions is a kind of shorthand for talking about the medicinal properties of a plant. Knowing how to choose the best herb or how to create an herbal remedy that combines a variety of actions are skills that may take years to master. As you become more familiar with the medicinal characteristics of each plant, it will be easier to choose plants based on their known actions. Actions are general guidelines; they're listed in approximate descending order of importance, even though many herbs have several actions that are equally important. For more information about the language of herbal actions, please refer to one of the general herb primers in the Bibliography. The Glossary contains definitions of key actions.

★ Part Used

Before harvesting or buying herbs, it's important to know exactly which part of the plant contains the healing action you need. Parts generally used are: the root, rhizome, leaf, flower, leaf with flower, flowering tops, bark, and the seeds or fruits.

Be aware that different parts of the same plant may have very different actions. For example, the leaf of the plant may be used to soothe skin irritation while the root of the same plant may induce vomiting. For most herbs, there is an official part used in modern herbal practice, and this is the part often sold commercially. Folk tradition may have relied on entirely different parts of the plant. Although any parts of a plant may have some medicinal actions, these other parts are often less potent than the official part. Some parts of a plant may have little or no medicinal value.

★ Traditional and Current Uses

A plant's historical use often reveals what its role may be in healing current health challenges. One hundred years ago in Western culture, the emphasis was on using herbs to manage infectious diseases like influenza and pneumonia. Many of today's health problems result from the long-term effects of stress and environmental toxins. The herbs now in demand are those that treat insomnia, depression, and immune system problems.

Fortunately, there is plenty of ethnobotanical documentation about how indigenous peoples used southern Appalachian medicinal plants and about the Europeans' discovery of many of the same plants. While cultural bias often skews the accuracy of this information, we can still discern familiar patterns that provide important information about these plants' essential character as medicines.

In more recent times, an extensive record of information about the traditional folk uses of herbs in the Appalachians comes from the work of Alabama herbalist A. L. Tommie Bass. Mr. Bass, who died in 1996, was a successful herbalist who used over 300 herbs in his practice. His use of medicinal herbs has been documented in several excellent books by Crellin, Philpott, and Patton that were referenced in the writing of this book. (*See* Notes.)

As modern translators of historical information, we have an opportunity to use herbs in new ways, thus making our own contribution to the living art of herbalism. Information about the plants' traditional and current uses is offered only as a starting point for your experience of the plants.

★ Harvesting

Information about when and how to harvest medicinal plants is an important part of the tradition that herbalists have handed down for generations, because knowing how to use plants that were harvested at the appropriate time is the basis of creating effective herbal medicines. The ideal time of harvest varies from plant to plant, because the medicinal compounds in plants change during various stages of the growth cycle. For example, a newly emerging leaf usually contains more active chemical compounds in early spring than it does later in the growing season after the plant has flowered and gone to seed. Careful observation is needed to track the growth cycle of plants through the seasons. In general, if a plant is harvested at the correct time and carefully processed, its medicinal actions remain very strong. Plants harvested before or after their peak make poor quality medicines.

Harvesting instructions are based on each plant's botanical characteristics. You'll find bloom and harvest calendars in the back of this book. They should help you with plant identification and give you some idea of when the plant is harvested. The appropriate harvesting time may vary slightly from year to year and according to the weather in the region where the plant is growing. Proper harvesting instructions are included, such as "dig the entire root after the first frost" or "collect the leaves before the flowers appear." Various cultures use time-honored methods of determining when to harvest, such as the phases of the moon and other astrological, astronomical, and environmental signs. You may need a season or two of observing a plant before you get in sync with the rhythms of its growth cycle.

If you are new to wild plant identification, you may want to find an experienced herbalist or native plant enthusiast willing to assist you in learning how to identify plants. Basic botany books and field guides with identification keys are helpful, but it is often preferable to learn the subtleties of plant identification in the field.

Detailed instructions are given here about when to harvest each plant for peak medicinal potency. Before collecting any plants, be certain you know exactly what part of the plant is medicinal. This book contains information about how to harvest each plant without destroying it unless, of course, it is the root that is collected. Even then, it is sometimes possible to replant a section of the root or rhizome, or ripe seed, so that the plant will regenerate itself. For more propagation information, please see the Bibliography.

When preparing to go on a harvesting expedition, assemble and pack everything you'll need to store the plants after they are harvested. Pack labels and a pen, along with paper bags. As you harvest each plant, place each species in its own labeled bag; once plants wilt, they all look remarkably similar. Avoid using plastic bags, because plants stored in plastic quickly become mush. It is always a good idea to wear gloves when harvesting fresh plants.

Frequent contact with fresh plants can cause skin irritation and other unpleasant symptoms.

★ Ethical Harvesting Methods

Large quantities of medicinal plants have been over-harvested from the southern Appalachians for hundreds of years. The number of plants in the forest today is a mere shadow of the abundance that once existed. Threats to the survival of wild plant populations have increased over the last 30 years due to the renewed interest in botanical medicines and the large-scale manufacture of herbal products. The surge in environmental destruction to fragile mountain ecosystems has also contributed to a state of emergency for wild plant populations.

Because many of the plants included here are only found in the wild—they will not grow outside their native habitat or are not being cultivated—it is critical that you only harvest plants from land you have studied carefully. Tim Blakely, one of my first herb teachers, advises everyone to observe wild plants in a particular place for at least one year before deciding to harvest them. Tim believes that until you're able to see whether a plant is part of a community of plants thriving from year to year, you can't predict how your harvesting some of the plants will affect the well-being of all those that remain.

Several guidelines to follow when ethically harvesting wild plants:

❧ Do not harvest on private property without permission of the owner. You could be prosecuted for theft or trespassing. If you are interested in harvesting plants on private property, introduce yourself to the landowner and explain what you would like to do and why. Although they will probably think you are crazy to be collecting plants to use as medicine, if you reassure landowners that you will collect the plants without damaging their property, most are willing to let you help yourself to their abundant supply of weeds.

◗ Do not collect plants from national or state parks or forests, recreation areas, wildlife management areas, nature preserves, etc. This land is held in the public trust, and removing plants is strictly prohibited and punishable by a fine. In some areas, permits are issued for collecting specific medicinal plants from public lands. Inquire at the local U. S. Forest Service or State Parks office for details.

◗ Do not collect plants from along roadways, railway lines, beneath electrical lines or from any other areas that are routinely sprayed with or exposed to toxic chemicals. Do not harvest any plant that you can see from a car, because it will have been regularly exposed to toxic gasoline fumes.

◗ Before harvesting any wild plants, verify their official conservation status by checking the plant's botanical name against lists published by various state and federal agencies or local conservation groups.

Several excellent conservation groups carefully monitor medicinal plant populations in the eastern United States and can provide helpful information. One recommended group is United Plant Savers, an organization dedicated to preserving and protecting native medicinal plants in North America.

If there is a native plant society or wildflower group in your area, it also may be a reliable source of native plant information. In addition, don't forget botanical gardens; they often sponsor symposia and lectures about regional plants. Many botanical gardens feature well-labeled collections of native plants and may know of local conservation groups that sponsor plant rescues to remove native plants from land scheduled for development. Participating in plant rescues can be heartbreaking but is also a great way to relocate native plants to safeguard their survival. More information about these groups may be found in the Resources section.

✹ Herbal Preparations

Making herbal medicines can be very satisfying. There is a wonderful sense of accomplishment that comes from looking at a cupboard in your home lined with jars full of dried herbs for teas, bottles of honey-rich cough syrup, potent tinctures and skin salves. For each plant included here, you will find ways to make herbal preparations that are based upon historical and current use. For the most part, medicine making requires a small investment in tools and supplies and yields a handsome return. For detailed instructions, see Chapter 2: The Simple Art of Medicine Making.

✹ Treatment and Dosages

The information in this book is based upon the assumption that the reader has a basic understanding of herbalism. If you are new to working with plant medicines, before you use any of the plants described here, please see Resources for a list of excellent herbals that give detailed information about basic herbal thera-peutics. See the Therapeutic Index for specific information on choosing herbs to treat individual symptoms and diseases.

Dosages given throughout this book are approximations based on my clinical experience and information I've gathered from other experienced practitioners and herbal reference books. This information should be considered a general guideline for creating herbal therapies. Though this information is considered to be accurate, it should not be used as a substitute for advice from a trained health care practitioner.

The Simple Art of Medicine Making

Making medicines for home use is no more complicated than cooking a meal. All you need are the right tools, the freshest ingredients, and a clearly written, easy-to-follow recipe along with the willingness to learn from your mistakes. The information given here will help you to get started.

✱ Herbal Teas (Infusions and Decoctions)

There are two classifications of medicinal teas: infusions and decoctions. If an herb is steeped in hot or cold water, it is an infusion. If the herb is boiled or simmered in water, it is a decoction. Delicate or aromatic parts of plants, such as flowers and leaves, are infused. Woody, fibrous parts of plants, such as roots, seeds, and barks, are decocted. When both types of plant parts are used, each type is prepared separately and then combined.

The ratio of herb to water used to make a medicinal tea is much greater than the ratio used to make a beverage tea; as a result, medicinal tea has a strong, distinctive flavor. Many of the most effective herbal remedies include bitter or harsh-tasting herbs. Feel free to sweeten medicinal tea with a small amount of honey or dilute with water or fruit juice, unless other instructions for use are given. Avoid the use of refined sugar or artificial sweet-eners.

I prefer the weight-to-volume method of preparing medicinal teas. To use this method, you will need a measuring cup and a scale that indicates weight in ounces. As a general rule, use two parts fresh herb or one part dry herb to 16 parts water. An easy way to translate this is to use 2 ounces of fresh herb or 1 ounce of dry herb for 16 ounces of water. Due to their relatively short shelf life, medicinal teas are usually made once a day to provide several doses at one time. To get the correct ratios of herb to water the first few times you use this method, I recommend that you use a scale to weigh the herbs and a measuring cup for the water. After that, you may be able to judge the amounts needed for the correct ratio just by looking.

To make an infusion, place fresh or dried herbs in a teapot or in a one-quart canning jar. Add boiling water. Cover and steep as indicated for each herb. Strain out the spent herb and discard. Store infusions in the refrigerator and use within 24 hours.

To make a decoction, place fresh or dry herbs in a non-aluminum pot with a lid, add cold water, and bring to a boil. Immediately reduce the heat; cover and simmer for 20 minutes or as indicated for each herb. Cool the decoction; strain out the spent herb and discard. Always start with cold water when making a decoction. Immersing herbs in hot water causes the cell walls to contract, which reduces solubility and results in a weaker prepara-tion. Store decoctions in the refrigerator and use within 24 hours. Drink infusions or decoctions at room temperature or as recom-mended for each herb.

Remember that the weight-to-volume measurements given here are to be used as a general guideline. For the best results, use the specific recommendations for individual herbs.

✹ Tinctures (Alcohol Extracts)

The process of making a tincture, or alcohol extract, is simple. An herb is soaked in a solvent, usually some kind of liquor like vodka or high quality brandy—not rubbing alcohol—that is a combination of alcohol (ethanol) and water, for at least two weeks.

The solvent, which is called the menstruum, can be any 80 or 100 proof liquor or grain alcohol, including moonshine. Although, technically speaking, distillation of grains into alcohol is illegal without a permit, in an emergency when store-bought alcohol is not available, home-distilled alcohol can be used as a substitute for grain alcohol.

The herb is extracted, or macerated, into the menstruum for two weeks. Finally, the herbs are pressed, or squeezed, out of the menstruum. The spent herbs, known as the marc, are discarded. The liquid extract or tincture is stored in a sterile bottle. No heat is involved in making tinctures.

A menstruum is always a combination of alcohol and water. The ratio of alcohol to water needed varies according to the chemical make-up of individual plants. For example, in order to break down herbs that have high resin content, such as sweet gum, a menstruum that is composed almost completely of alcohol is needed. Conversely, skullcap, an herb traditionally prepared as a tea, is almost completely soluble in water. Therefore, the amount of alcohol needed to make a skullcap tincture is very low. To safely preserve a tincture, it must contain a minimum of 25 percent alcohol. For health and economic reasons when making tinctures, always use as little alcohol as possible. Tinctures have a shelf life of five years or more.

When making tinctures, there is no official standard for determining the perfect ratio of alcohol and water to use. Experienced tincture makers develop custom menstruums for each individual herb, sometimes using different ratios for different batches of herbs. In a way, trying to determine the perfect menstruum ratio for each herb is a bit like asking if there is one particular way to make soup; ratios will vary according to the ingredients and the preferences of the cook. What is most important is that the final product—the soup—is delicious and nourishing, or the tincture is an effective medicine. In this book, the menstruum recommendations for each herb are based on my experience and on information I've gleaned from other experienced herbal medicine makers. This information is only a jumping off point for you to use in developing your own experience of making herbal tinctures.

A simple method of computing menstruum ratios is to use a standard menstruum: a combination of 50 percent alcohol and 50 percent water. Standard menstruums produce a good tincture for most herbs. However, if you are working with a rare or costly herb and want to be sure you achieve the most potent results, you may want to create a custom menstruum.

An easy way to get a standard menstruum is to use 100 proof liquor. The proof of the liquor, divided by two, gives you the ratio of alcohol it contains: 100 proof liquor is 50 percent alcohol and 50 percent water. 80 proof liquor is 40 percent alcohol and 60 percent water. It's fine to use any type of liquor with the correct proof, although vodka is often preferred, because it has fewer additives and little flavor.

If the recommended menstruum calls for anything other than 40 percent or 50 percent alcohol, you must use grain alcohol and dilute it with water to make a custom menstruum. Grain alcohol is 190 proof; it contains 95 percent alcohol and 5 percent water.

The chart on page 29 will help you to calculate the amount of grain alcohol and water needed to make custom menstruums. For best results when using custom menstruums, first make up a quantity of menstruum in a large container. Then, add the amount of menstruum needed to the herbs. Alcohol and water ratios are given in ounces.

✶ Making Tinctures

There are two methods of making tinctures by extraction: the folk method and the weight-to-volume method. The folk method is one of the oldest ways to preserve herbs. The weight-to-volume method is a more scientific method and uses weights and measures.

The folk method is easy but not cost-effective, because it produces a small amount of tincture for the quantity of herbs used. The weight-to-volume method results in the maximum amount of tincture for the quantity of herbs used. It is based on international pharmaceutical standards for tincture making. Commercial medicine makers use the weight-to-volume method along with custom menstruums created for each herb.

✶ Folk Tinctures

To make a tincture using the folk method, place chopped fresh herbs or ground dried herbs in a one-quart canning jar. Herbs should fill the jar snugly but not be tightly packed. Pour in the menstruum—standard or custom—until it is about two inches above the level of the herbs. Cap the jar and shake it well. Store it in a cool, dark place for two weeks. Once or twice a day, give the jar a good energetic shake so that the herbs really dance around in the menstruum.

After two weeks, the tincture is ready. Strain the entire contents of the jar through a colander lined with cotton muslin into a large bowl. Cut the muslin to a size large enough to drape over the sides of the colander. Allow the tincture to drain through the fabric-lined colander for a few minutes and then gather up the edges of the muslin to form a small pouch of wet herbs. Hold the pouch over a bowl. With one hand, hold the top of the pouch together. With the other hand, squeeze out all the liquid from the herbs and discard the spent marc. Pour the tincture from the bowl into a clean glass jar, cap, and label. Store in a cool, dark place.

✹ Weight-to-Volume Tinctures

To make a tincture using the weight-to-volume method, you must first calculate the amount of herbs you have, because the amount of herbs is what determines the amount of menstruum needed. Fresh herbs are tinctured at a ratio of one part herb to two parts menstruum. Dry herbs require a ratio of one part herb to five parts menstruum. Some very strong herbs are tinctured at a ratio of one part herb to 10 parts menstruum. These herbs are sometimes referred to as toxic, but I prefer to think of them as dosage specific or low-dose medicines that require more dilute tincture preparations and careful attention to dosage. Herbs are calculated by weight, while the amount of menstruum, being liquid, is measured by volume.

First, weigh the herbs on a scale. Before weighing, fresh herbs should be completely clean and cut into small pieces or chopped finely, and dried herbs should be ground into a powder. To grind dried herbs, use an electric coffee mill (reserved only for use with herbs) or a sturdy mortar and pestle. Place the weighed herbs in a jar or other glass container. A quart jar works fine unless you are making larger quantities.

Use the Weight-to-Volume Chart (page 28) to calculate the amount of menstruum needed based on the weight of the herbs. If you are using a custom menstruum, mix it according to the desired ratio of water to alcohol (see the Custom Menstruums Chart on page 29.)

Use a measuring cup to determine the correct amount of menstruum, and then pour the menstruum over the herbs. Fresh herbs may need to be processed in a blender or food processor with the menstruum so that they will be completely submerged in the liquid. Whether fresh or dried, the herbs must be submerged completely in the menstruum. Cap the jar and shake well. Store tincture in a cool, dark place for at least two weeks. Once or twice a day, give the jar a good energetic shake, so that the herbs really dance around in the menstruum.

After the tincture has steeped, or macerated, for two weeks, it is ready to strain. Strain the entire contents of the jar through a colander lined with cotton muslin into a large bowl. Cut the muslin to a size large enough to drape over the sides of the colander. Allow the tincture to drain for a few minutes through the fabric-lined colander and then gather up the edges of the muslin to form a small pouch of wet herbs. Hold the pouch over a bowl. With one hand, hold the top of the pouch together. With the other hand, squeeze out all the liquid from the herbs and discard the spent marc. Pour the tincture from the bowl into a clean glass jar.

If bits of herb have managed to escape the muslin and are now floating around in the tincture, you will need to filter the mixture once more. The best way to do this is by using a paper coffee filter and a freestanding coffee-filter holder placed over a clean quart jar. Before you begin, pour a cup of boiling water through the filter. Hot water is needed to get the filter to expand. Empty the boiling water from the quart jar before proceeding.

Weight-to-Volume Method

Weight-to-Volume Method - Ratio of Herb to Menstruum		
Fresh herbs	1:2	1 part herb to 2 parts menstruum (herb weight x 2 = volume of menstruum)
Dry herbs	1:5	1 part herb to 5 parts menstruum (herb weight x 5 = volume of menstruum)
Dosage Specific Herbs (Dried Herbs Only)	1:10	1 part herb to 10 parts menstruum (herb weight x 10 = volume of menstruum)

Use this chart to determine the proper ratio of herbs to menstruum needed to make a tincture.

Custom Menstruums Chart

Quantity of Menstruum Needed	Grain Alcohol to Water Ratios for Custom Menstruums							
	50%		60%		70%		80%	
	GA	water	GA	water	GA	water	GA	water
4	2	2	2.5	1.5	3	1	3.5	0.5
8	4	4	5	3	6	2	7	1
12	6	6	8	4	9	3	10	2
16	8	8	10	6	12	4	13.5	2.5

All measurements in ounces.

Use this chart to calculate out the correct ratio of grain alcohol to water needed to create a custom menstruum.

★ Simple Syrup

Simple syrup combines a very strong herbal tea with an equal amount of honey. Do not make syrups using refined sugar. Refined sugar and artificial sweeteners disrupt immune response, while honey enhances the effectiveness of herbs as a treatment for sore throats, coughs, and stomach upsets.

The first step is to make a strong infusion. You may use one herb or a combination of herbs. For each quart of water, use two ounces of dried herb or four ounces of fresh herb. Bruise and chop fresh herbs or grind dry herbs, then weigh them. Place the prepared herbs in a non-aluminum pot with a tight-fitting lid. Bring the correct amount of water to a boil in a separate pot and then pour the boiling water over the herbs. Cover and infuse for six hours or overnight. After the infusion is complete, bring the mixture to a boil and simmer, covered, for 20 minutes. Remove from the heat and cool.

Strain the herbs by pouring the mixture through a colander lined with a piece of cotton muslin. Squeeze the muslin to get out every drop of liquid. Discard spent herbs. Measure the herb mixture and pour into a clean pot; cover and bring to a boil. Reduce the heat and simmer until the volume reduces by half. Let the concentrated decoction cool for 10 minutes. While it is still warm, measure it and return it to the pot. For each ounce of decoction, add one-half ounce of honey and stir until the honey dissolves completely. Cool and pour it into sterile bottles. Refrigerate. Customize your syrup by adding brandy, herbal tinctures, lemon or lime juice, or a few drops of any essential oil used to treat respiratory symptoms. If properly stored, syrups have a shelf life of one year. Check for spoilage before using. Spoiled syrup will be moldy or cloudy.

✳ Compress

A compress is a hot, moist cloth soaked in a hot or cold herbal infusion or decoction and applied to the skin. Prepare an herbal infusion or decoction as indicated for individual herbs.

Compresses may be used to increase blood circulation; warm stiff muscles and joints; break up congestion in the lungs or sinuses; relieve back pain, muscle spasm or inflammation; cool a fever; bring boils to a head; or dissolve cysts or tumors.

To make a compress, brew a standard infusion or decoction using one or more herbs. Strain and discard the herbs. To make a hot compress, place the herbal mixture into a deep, wide non-aluminum pot with a tight-fitting lid, and heat almost to a boil. Remove from heat. Soak a small towel or other soft absorbent cloth in the hot herb mixture for a few minutes. Wring the cloth out and fold it so that it will completely cover the affected area. Apply to the skin and cover the compress with a dry towel to keep it warm. When the hot compress begins to cool, replace it with a fresh hot one.

To make a cool compress, allow the prepared herb mixture to cool completely before using. Soak a small towel or other absorbent cloth in the cool mixture. Wring out the cloth and fold it so that it will completely cover the affected area. Apply to the skin and cover the compress with a dry towel to keep from causing a chill. When the cool compress begins to get warm, replace it with a fresh cool one.

Repeat as needed. Treatment time should be at least 20 minutes or as indicated for the herbs used in the compress.

✳ Poultice

A poultice is a messy but effective way to use herbs topically to heal the skin, relieve inflammation, or stimulate circulation. To make a poultice of fresh herbs, pound freshly harvested leaves with a mortar and pestle or in a bowl with a wooden spoon, until they form a juicy pulp. If using dry herbs, place them directly in a small bowl and add hot water a little at a time until the herbs stick together. If the plants are too dry, add a little aloe vera gel until they hold together.

Loosely wrap the moistened herbs in a piece of cheesecloth so that the mixture is easier to work with or apply the herb directly to skin. Cover the herb poultice with a small piece of plastic. Place a dry towel on top of the plastic. On top of the towel, place a hot water bottle. To avoid irritation when using harsh or stimulating herbs, rub some olive oil on the skin before applying the poultice. Treatment time should be at least 20 minutes. Repeat as needed.

✹ Bath

All sorts of conditions may be treated by freshly brewed herbal infusions and decoctions added to a bath. This method is very effective for the relief of symptoms such as nausea or vomiting, as a relaxant for insomnia or anxiety, to treat skin problems, and when administering herbs to young children.

Make a standard infusion or decoction. You will need at least one quart. Strain, and pour into a warm or hot bath. Soak for 20 minutes. Prepare foot and hand baths in the same way.

✹ Enema

Use enemas sparingly to treat acute symptoms. Enemas provide immediate relief for constipation caused by illness, travel or medications. An enema may be used to administer herbal therapies that would otherwise be given orally to someone who is too weak to drink or unable to hold down fluids. Prepared with relaxing herbs, an enema may help to relieve pain, muscle spasm, anxiety and insomnia. Long-term use of enemas to treat constipation is not recommended. Avoid using any herb that might irritate mucus membranes.

Prepare a standard infusion or decoction and allow it to cool to body temperature before using. For best results, follow the directions included with enema bags.

✳ Vaginal Douche

Use an herbal douche to treat vaginal irritation, inflammation or infection. Prepare a standard infusion or decoction and cool to body temperature before using. For best results, follow the directions included with a douche bag. Avoid using any herb that might irritate mucus membranes.

Long-term use of douches is not recommended.

✳ Infused Herbal Oil

Medicinal properties of herbs may be extracted into vegetable oils. Prepare herbal oils by infusing fresh or dry herbs in warm vegetable oil. Use herbal oils externally to treat conditions such as dry skin, wounds, bruises, skin problems, and sore muscles. Here are two methods for making infused oils. The first, the solar infusion method, uses heat from the sun over several days to extract the herbs into vegetable oil. Obviously, either hot weather or exposure to direct sunlight is necessary to make a solar infusion. An infused oil made by the second, the oven method, is ready in only a few hours.

Infused oil may be made using any kind of quality vegetable oil, preferably organic. Some oils, such as olive or almond, stay on the skin for a long time and should be used when treating wounds, rashes, dryness, and other skin problems. Other oils, like grape seed, are quickly absorbed into the skin and should be used for treating bruises and sore muscles.

If fresh herbs are used to make oil infusions, be certain that the plants are completely dry. After harvesting, if possible, allow them to wilt for a few hours or overnight before using. If dry herbs are used, grind them into a coarse powder using a clean electric coffee mill.

Because infused oils are very susceptible to bacterial growth that causes rancidity, sterile jars should be used for making and storing them. To discourage bacterial growth in the mixture, choose a jar size that will hold the infused oil with little or no air space between the oil and the lid. Discard oils if they become cloudy or develop a rancid odor.

★ Solar-Infused Oil

To make solar-infused oil, place powdered dry herbs or chopped fresh herbs into a sterile jar. Pour enough vegetable oil into the jar to cover the herbs so that little or no air space remains between the mixture and the top of the jar. The herbs should not be tightly packed; they must be able to move around freely in the oil.

Use a chopstick or butter knife to poke down into the herbs and release any air bubbles. Cap tightly and shake well. Place the jar in a brown paper bag and set it outside in a place that receives direct sunlight for five or more hours a day. Shake the jar well at least once a day for three to five days. When the oil has a deep, rich color, it is ready. Carefully watch and smell oils during the infusion process. If mold or a rancid odor occurs, the oil must be discarded.

★ Oven Method Infused Oil

To use the oven method, carefully chop fresh herbs, or grind dry herbs into a coarse powder using an electric coffee mill. Spread the herbs evenly across the bottom of a two-quart ceramic or enameled casserole dish with a lid.

Slowly add enough oil to cover the herbs completely. Cover and bake at 250 degrees Fahrenheit (176 degrees Celsius) for one to two hours. Every 20 minutes or so, remove the lid from the dish and stir the mixture. Oils made with dry herbs require less cooking time than those made of fresh herbs. Remove the oil from the oven when it has a rich green color. Cool for about 20 minutes and strain.

To remove the spent herbs from infused oil, set a colander lined with cotton muslin over a large clean bowl. The size of the muslin should be big enough to drape over the sides of the colander. Pour the oil infusion into the colander; let it drain for about five minutes into the bowl, and then gather together the edges of the cloth and squeeze out the remaining oil.

Pour the strained oil into a sterile jar and cap it. Allow to sit undisturbed overnight. In the morning, slowly pour the oil into another sterile jar, being careful not to stir up any plant residue that will have settled to the bottom of the first jar. Discard the remaining plant residue. Store the infused oil in a cool, dark place or in the refrigerator. Herbal oils have a shelf life of one year.

❧ Herbal Salves

Salves are infused herbal oils thickened with beeswax and used topically to heal wounds, skin abrasions, dry skin or rashes. The combination of herbal oils and beeswax promotes healing by holding the medicinal properties of the herbs on the surface of the skin.

To make an herbal salve, measure several ounces of herbal oil into a non-aluminum pan. Warm the oil over a low heat for several minutes. Do not leave the oil unattended or overheat it.

Add one tablespoon of grated beeswax for each ounce of oil used, and stir until the wax completely dissolves. Remove pan from the heat. Test consistency of the oil and beeswax mixture by scooping up a spoonful of the mixture and allowing it to cool completely. For a faster way to test salve consistency, place a spoonful of the warm mixture on a plate and cool in the freezer for five minutes.

When the balance of oil and wax is correct, the cool salve should be easy to scoop up with your finger but not runny or oily. If the salve is too soft, add a little more grated beeswax to the oil in the pan. If too hard, thin with a little more oil. Pour into small, sterile wide-mouth jars and cool completely.

The Medicinal Plants

Bethroot

COMMON NAME: Bethroot

BOTANICAL NAME: *Trillium erectum*

FAMILY: *Liliaceae* (Lily)

OTHER NAMES: Red trillium, birthroot, wake-robin

RELATED SPECIES: *T. grandiflorum, T. catesbaei,* and other species

DESCRIPTION: Bethroot is one of the most easily identified early spring wildflowers; these hardy perennials are a living tribute to the number three: all floral parts grow in threes. Look for three sepals that surround three petals, which enclose two whorls of three stamens, three stigmas, and finally, three seeds.

Bethroot, or red trillium, has a single erect stem approximately one foot tall with three deep green triangular-oval leaves covered with a net-like pattern of veins. The solitary flower, which blooms between April and June, has lance-shaped petals that vary in color from a rich wine-red to pale pink and sometimes to white. The ovaries at the center of the flower are maroon-brown. Vasey's trillium (*T. vaseyi*), once considered a variety of *T. erectum*, has a similar flower that is larger and tends to hang face down, slightly hidden below the leaves. Many species of *Trillium* are found in the forests of the southern Appalachians.

MPH: pp. 157-158.

HABITAT: Deciduous forests. Botanists believe that the trillium genera are a remnant of an ancient forest that extended millions of years ago across North America and into eastern Asia. Once widespread in forests between the Atlantic and the Mississippi, *Trillia* are becoming rare due to the habitat disruption. Look for trillium near bloodroot (*Sanguinaria canadensis*), foam flower (*Tiarella cordifolia*), hepatica (*Hepatica acutiloba*), and other spring ephemerals.

KEY ACTIONS: Astringent, uterine tonic, expectorant

PART USED: Root, sometimes leaf

TRADITIONAL USES: Bethroot is an important part of the diverse American Indian apothecary of herbs used as labor tonics. The common name "bethroot" is derived from the more accurate name, birthroot, because it was often combined with black cohosh (*Actaea racemosa*) and blue cohosh (*Caulophyllum thalictroides*) to stimulate uterine contractions and promote labor. At the end of the 19th century, bethroot was a great favorite of Eclectic physicians who based their medical practice on the use of indigenous plant remedies and frequently used it in formulas to strengthen the female reproductive system.

   Bethroot also has a long history of use as a folk remedy for treating chronic respiratory problems including coughs, congestion, breathing difficulties, and asthma. It was used as an astringent to relieve diarrhea, hemorrhage, and excessive mucus secretions. A poultice of fresh leaf and root was applied to tumors, slow healing ulcers, insect bites, and gangrenous conditions.

CURRENT USES: Due to the declining populations of bethroot in the wild, combined with a slow propagation rate, bethroot is not widely available on the commercial herb market. As a labor stimulant, small amounts of root tincture are used by experienced herbalists and midwives. In respiratory formulas, it acts as a stimulating expectorant and helps to reduce lung congestion and inflammation. Bethroot is used in acute formulas to reduce heavy menstrual bleeding or to stop excessive diarrhea.

HARVESTING: The root is harvested after the flower fades in early summer.

PREPARATIONS: Only use bethroot from ethically harvested or cultivated sources.

♦ TINCTURE: Fresh root – 1:2. Menstruum – 70% alcohol.

♦ DECOCTION: Use one teaspoon dried or two teaspoons fresh root for each cup of water. Bring to a boil; cover and simmer for 10 minutes. Strain.

DOSAGES: Use bethroot with extreme caution; small doses are quite powerful. Before using, seek guidance from a practitioner familiar with the clinical use of this herb.

♦ TINCTURE: Take 10 to 20 drops three times a day or as recommended.

♦ DECOCTION: Take one-half cup of decoction three times a day or as needed to relieve symptoms.

Black Cohosh

COMMON NAME: Black Cohosh

BOTANICAL NAME: *Actaea racemosa* (syn. *Cimicifuga racemosa*)

FAMILY: *Ranunculaceae* (Buttercup)

OTHER NAMES: Black snakeroot, bugbane, bugwort, rattlewort, faerie torches

DESCRIPTION: Black cohosh is a beautiful perennial plant, two to three feet tall, with lush, dark green foliage and an airy, graceful appearance. Leaves have deeply divided, toothed leaflets, usually with three leaflets on each stem. There is a black mark on the stem where it forks into three branches.

In early summer a stately flower stalk, which may be solitary or branched, rises four to seven feet high from the center of the plant. Evenly spaced buds that resemble peas emerge along the upper portions of the flower stalk and remain unopened for a month or more. In late June or early July, the flowers begin to bloom from bottom to top. The delicate white flower is composed of a cluster of stamens surrounding a rather fat, short stigma. Tiny sepals fall off soon after blooming. The common name, faerie torches, is an apt description, because the elegant black cohosh flowers look like a luminous flame glowing in the deep shade of the forest. The fragrance of the flower is unpleasant.

MPH: pp. 64-65.

Black Cohosh - Actaea racemosa

HABITAT: Found on slopes in the deep shade of deciduous forests.

KEY ACTIONS: Nervine, anti-spasmodic, anti-inflammatory, anti-rheumatic, emmenagogue, sedative

PART USED: Root

TRADITIONAL USES: American Indians soaked black cohosh roots in alcohol to make a remedy for rheumatic pain. It was also used to treat coughs and colds, bring on delayed menses, and to help babies sleep.[2]

CURRENT USES: Black cohosh is one of the most effective herbs used to treat menstrual and menopausal discomfort. It relieves menstrual pain and cramping, irritability, and headaches. It is used extensively to relieve menopausal symptoms such as insomnia, anxiety, nervousness, depression, hot flashes, and skin-crawling sensations. Black cohosh is also useful in the treatment of uterine pain, endometriosis, and post-partum depression.

It relieves pain and inflammation caused by arthritis, rheumatism, and fibromyalgia, and relaxes spasmodic coughs caused by colds, bronchitis, and whooping cough.

HARVESTING: In the late summer or early fall, dig black cohosh roots after the flowers have faded. The foliage seems to die back suddenly, making identification difficult late in the growing season. However, if you look for the faded flower stalk covered with round, dried seed pods, black cohosh can often be harvested into autumn. Ideally, black cohosh is harvested before the first frost.

Black cohosh roots form a thick twisted bundle that is challenging to clean. To loosen dirt, cut roots apart and soak in water for a short time. Clean and scrub the roots with a small vegetable brush and lots of patience. Sort through cleaned roots and discard woody or blackened parts. Immediately tincture fresh roots. To dry for future use, cut the roots into slices about one-half inch thick and allow to dry completely before storing. Black cohosh will mold if not carefully dried. White "buds" found along the rootstock will provide the next year's growth. These chlorophyll-free nodules, along with a few inches of the rootstock, can be replanted to produce a new plant.

Black cohosh is sometimes confused with the look-alike white baneberry or doll's eyes (*Actaea alba*, or *A. pachypoda*) that has similar foliage. A significant difference is the arrangement of the flowers and the colors of the berries. The flowers of black cohosh grow along a tall, slender raceme that can be a foot or more tall. Berries are dark purple. In contrast, the flowers of white baneberry grow in a tight, short raceme close to the leaves, and the berries are white with a dark purple mark or "eye." White baneberry is toxic and not safe for medicinal use.

PREPARATIONS:

 TINCTURE: Fresh root – 1:2. Dried root – 1:5. Menstruum – 60% alcohol.

 DECOCTION: Use one teaspoon dried or two teaspoons fresh root for each cup of water. Bring to a boil; cover and simmer for ten minutes. Strain.

DOSAGES: Only use recommended dosage. High doses of black cohosh may cause dizziness, frontal headache, nausea and even vomiting. Reduce dosage or discontinue use if any of these symptoms occur.

 TINCTURE: Take 20 to 40 drops every hour for acute symptoms or three times a day as a tonic.

♦ DECOCTION: Drink one-half cup of decoction every two hours as needed for acute symptoms or one and a half cups total decoction per day as a tonic.

Black Haw

COMMON NAME: Black Haw

BOTANICAL NAME: *Viburnum prunifolium*

FAMILY: *Caprifoliaceae* (Honeysuckle)

OTHER NAMES: Crampbark, arrow-wood, snowball plant

RELATED SPECIES: Possum haw (*V. nudum*), crampbark (*V. opulus*)

DESCRIPTION: Black haw is a small, deciduous shrub or tree, three to six feet tall, with finely serrated, oval, opposite leaves and bunches of small white flowers that bloom in flat clusters during April and May. Historically, the straight, smooth branches were used to make arrows, hence the common name, arrow-wood. In the late summer, small dark blue-black berries or "haws" appear.
    MPH: p. 277.

HABITAT: Commonly found in the understory of deciduous forests, along creek banks and at the edges of open, sunny areas.

KEY ACTIONS: Anti-spasmodic, anti-inflammatory, astringent

PART USED: Bark

Black Haw - Viburnum prunifolium

TRADITIONAL USES: Black haw was a common ingredient in formulas for women's "monthly troubles" and was used to relieve menstrual cramps, prevent miscarriage and as a labor tonic during the last few weeks of pregnancy. It was an ingredient in one of the best selling herbal remedies of all times, "Lydia Pinkham's Vegetable Compound for Females." Black haw was also used to relieve nervousness, stomach cramps, and tics or spasm.

CURRENT USES: Black haw is a reliable remedy to relieve cramps or spasm anywhere in the body.

Because it works without causing drowsiness, it is useful in treating a wide range of symptoms. Frequent small doses relieve heart palpitations, arthritic, rheumatic or sciatic pain, breathing difficulties caused by asthma, and intestinal cramps caused by Irritable Bowel Syndrome and Crohn's disease. It is a reliable remedy for menstrual cramps, ovarian pain, and excessive menstrual bleeding. During labor, black haw helps to regulate uterine contractions and reduce post-partum bleeding.

The actions of black haw are interchangeable with those of crampbark (*Viburnum opulus*), an herb widely available on the commercial herb market. Crampbark is a shrub native to Europe and commonly used as a landscape plant.

HARVESTING: The best way to harvest black haw is to prune the outer branches in early spring as soon as the leaves emerge. If one cuts back only the branches, one or two plants are enough to provide an abundant source of medicine. At the same time, black haw will flourish from the annual pruning. Strip leaves off the cut branches; use a sharp knife to peel the bark into strips and discard the inner pith. Thin twigs, smaller than one-half inch in diameter, may be cut into one-inch slices and used without separating the bark from the pith. Tincture fresh bark or dry completely for future use.

PREPARATIONS:

◊ TINCTURE: Fresh bark – 1:2. Dried bark – 1:5. Menstruum – 50% alcohol.

◊ DECOCTION: Use two teaspoons dried or one teaspoon fresh bark for each cup of water. Bring to a boil; cover and simmer for 15 minutes. Strain.

DOSAGES: For the fastest results when treating acute symptoms, use small, frequent doses of tincture until symptoms improve. After this, reduce dosage frequency to every hour or more as needed.

◊ TINCTURE: Put one teaspoon tincture in one ounce of warm water; drink this every 20 minutes. Repeat until symptoms improve. Increase dosage to two teaspoons every 20 minutes if symptoms fail to improve after two to three doses.

◊ DECOCTION: Drink one-half cup of warm black haw decoction every 20 minutes until symptoms improve, then use as needed.

Black Walnut

COMMON NAME: Black Walnut

BOTANICAL NAME: *Juglans nigra*

FAMILY: *Juglandaceae* (Walnut)

OTHER NAMES: American walnut, walnut

DESCRIPTION: Black walnut is a large, deciduous tree, 25 to 100 feet tall, with deeply ridged, gray-black bark. Unisexual flowers, small inconspicuous female flowers on the ends of the branches and male flowers dangling in catkins, bloom April through June. Leaves emerge late in the spring and have a reddish-pink color when new. The compound leaves are composed of alternate leaflets, usually 12 to 24 per stem, that are finely toothed and about three inches in length. The green fruit is about the size of a tennis ball and grows singly or in clusters. As it ripens, the thick outer hull turns black and furrowed. Within the hull is a brown hard-shelled nut that contains delicious oil-rich black walnut meat. When green the hull has a pungent odor. The fresh hulls cause a long-lasting black stain on anything they touch.
MPH: pp. 310-311.

HABITAT: Throughout the region.

PART USED: Leaf, hull (root bark, bark)

KEY ACTIONS: Astringent, alterative, purgative, vermifuge, anti-fungal, antiseptic

TRADITIONAL USES: In American Indian and local folk medicine, black walnut leaves were decocted and used topically as an antiseptic wash for sores and skin infections. The leaves were dried, powdered, and mixed with table salt, and then applied to skin infections.[3] The juice of the black hull was believed to cure herpes, eczema, and ringworm. During the Civil War, black walnut leaves and bergamot oil were added to skin salves to treat infected sores. Leaves were also boiled and applied to the skin of horses and other animals to prevent flea bites.[4] Eclectic practitioners used black walnut root bark internally to heal intestinal irritation and inflammation of the intestines that resulted in diarrhea.

Black walnut meat is considered a delicacy. Black walnut hull is an important dye plant; the hulls are used to make a beautiful chocolate brown color, and the leaves produce a green dye.

CURRENT USES: Black walnut leaf and hull are standard in modern herbal practice. A strong, somewhat harsh remedy, it should be used with caution. Black walnut is often used as a small part of a larger formula so that its effects will be buffered by the actions of other herbs. Black walnut is used internally in formulas to treat systemic yeast infections (*Candidiasis*) and to eliminate intestinal worms and parasites. In small, regular doses, it is considered a blood cleansing tonic. It acts as a strong laxative in large doses. A wash or salve made from the green hulls treats ringworm, scabies, cradle cap, and fungal infections. The leaf decoction is used as a douche to relieve vaginal discharge or itching.

HARVESTING: Collect black walnut leaves in early summer before the fruits have fully formed.

Black walnut fruits usually fall to the ground while still green, in early autumn. Collect fruits as soon as they fall. To separate the hulls from the nuts, put the fruits in a burlap bag or gunny sack, securely close the bag and place it on a hard surface (a paved road or driveway). Drive the tire of a car back and forth over the bag to crack the hulls. Wearing waterproof gloves, separate the hulls from the nuts. Use a large hammer or mallet if necessary to crack the hulls open completely and to break them into smaller pieces. Dry the hulls or process them fresh.

Reserve the delicious black walnuts for eating after the nuts have seasoned a few weeks in a sunny dry place. Open the hard walnut shell with a hammer or a special black walnut cracking tool sold for this purpose. Do not store walnuts in the shell for more than a few weeks or they will develop worms.

PREPARATIONS:

◊ TINCTURE: Dried leaf – 1:5. Menstruum – 50% alcohol. Hull – 1:5. Menstruum – 65% alcohol.

◊ DECOCTION: Use one teaspoon dried leaves for each cup of water. Bring water to a boil; cover and simmer for 15 minutes. Strain. Decoct the green hulls by covering completely with water, bringing to a boil, and then simmering for 20 minutes. Strain and use as a skin wash.

◊ SALVE: Make a standard salve with infused oil made from fresh or dried black walnut leaves or green hulls. Some Southern folk recipes recommend boiling black walnut hulls in hog lard to make salve.

DOSAGES: Used internally, high doses of black walnut leaf or hull tincture can have a powerful purgative action, causing severe diarrhea or vomiting. Start with the lowest dose indicated, and do not exceed the highest dose. Use freely as a topical skin preparation.

- TINCTURE: Take 10 to 20 drops diluted in a small amount of water three times a day.

- DECOCTION: Drink one-half cup leaf decoction three times a day. Use hull decoction as a wash, compress or vaginal douche once or twice a day until symptoms improve.

- SALVE: Apply to affected area as needed.

Bloodroot

COMMON NAME: Bloodroot

BOTANICAL NAME: *Sanguinaria canadensis*

FAMILY: *Papaveraceae* (Poppy)

OTHER NAMES: Pucoon, red pucoon, Indian paint

DESCRIPTION: Bloodroot is one of the earliest blooming spring wildflowers. The waxy, white flower has golden yellow stamens at its center and blooms just above the leaf mulch in late March. From inside the reddish curled leaf, buds emerge with one flower on each stalk. The flower blooms briefly; as it fades, the leaf unfurls. The leaf of the bloodroot is an unusual palmate type described as 'irregularly lobed.' The shape of the leaf resembles a large green jigsaw puzzle piece. The entire plant ranges from four to six inches tall. The root is thick and fleshy, about the size and shape of a little finger. When the root is cut, bright red-orange juices are secreted. The juice is caustic and may cause skin irritation.
MPH: pp. 54-55.

HABITAT: Deciduous hardwood forests.

KEY ACTIONS: Expectorant, anti-spasmodic, anti-inflammatory, cathartic, emetic, escharotic, emmenagogue

PART USED: Root

TRADITIONAL USES: Bloodroot is one of the best known indigenous remedies in the Appalachians and throughout the Eastern States where it has a long history of use and was reputed to be an effective external treatment for cancerous growths. A paste of the fresh root, combined with other herbs, was applied to the skin and allowed to work for 24 hours. The effect was to burn away the skin and, hopefully, the cancerous growth. This method was also used to treat ulcers, warts, polyps, and fungal conditions. In the 19th century, a physician noted that bloodroot "cures or relieves pneumonic inflammation, while it checks or suppresses expectoration."[5] It was used, along with wild ginger, rabbit tobacco, wild cherry, and lobelia,[6] as a cough remedy for bronchial spasms. The powdered root was used as a snuff and thought to act as a tonic stimulant to reduce mucus in the lungs and sinuses.

In some parts of the Appalachians, bloodroot was considered to be a love charm with aphrodisiac powers. Tommie Bass noted that African Americans called it "coon root" and that they drank bloodroot-infused whiskey to "build a nature" (increase sex drive).[7]

CURRENT USES: Bloodroot tincture is used in formulas, usually with other expectorant and demulcent herbs, to relieve bronchitis, coughs, lung congestion and inflammation. Small doses of bloodroot relax the bronchial muscles and help ease breathing difficulties. At the same time, it acts as a stimulating expectorant to clear congestion from the lungs. It also reduces inflammation in the throat and chest, and relieves spasmodic coughs.

Low doses of bloodroot tincture (five to 10 drops in a small amount of water) may be used to warm the stomach to relieve symptoms of dampness such as indigestion, gas and bloating. The same treatment is used to stimulate bile secretions and to relieve liver congestion in the treatment of hepatitis and jaundice.

Bloodroot salve treats slow healing sores, ulcers, chronic eczema and warts. It is an ingredient in escharotic cancer salves used for purging tumors and basal cell carcinomas. (See the book, *Cancer Salves*, by Ingrid Naiman.) Fresh root poultice is used with caution to treat warts, fungal growths, and ringworm.

Today, bloodroot is used as an ingredient in commercial mouthwash and toothpaste to reduce gum inflammation and plaque build-up.

HARVESTING: Collect the root in early spring when the flower is in full bloom or in late summer as the leaves begin to fade. The fresh root can cause irritation and should be handled with care.

PREPARATIONS: Tinctures and salves are the standard methods of using this medicine. Tincture prepared with the fresh root is recommended. Use dried root when making infused oils. Traditionally, when bloodroot is used internally to treat lung congestion and coughs, it is in combination with other demulcent lung herbs such as mullein (*Verbascum thapsus*), plantain (*Plantago major*), or coltsfoot (*Tussilago farfara*). Bloodroot is usually less than one-eighth part of the total formula.

◖ Fresh root – 1:10. Menstruum – 50% alcohol.

◖ SALVE: Prepare a standard salve with infused bloodroot oil.

DOSAGES: Bloodroot requires careful attention to dosage. It is contraindicated during pregnancy or for use with children.

◖ TINCTURE: Take 10 drops of tincture diluted in half a cup of water three to four times a day. This preparation may also be used as mouthwash to treat gum inflammation or plaque.

◊ SALVES: Apply salve daily to the affected area and cover with a piece of cotton gauze. Bloodroot salves will cause some degree of inflammation.

Blue Cohosh

COMMON NAME: Blue Cohosh

BOTANICAL NAME: *Caulophyllum thalictroides*

FAMILY: *Berberidaceae* (Barberry)

DESCRIPTION: Blue cohosh is an airy, lush perennial about two feet tall that has compound leaves with two or three delicately lobed leaflets each. There is a blue-green cast to the underside of the leaves, in contrast with the green surface. Small, greenish-yellow flowers, composed of little sepals with even smaller petals at the base, appear in terminal clusters from April to June. The fruit is dark blue and about the size and color of a blueberry. It often remains after the foliage has died back in the fall.
MPH: pp. 233-234.

HABITAT: Deciduous forests. Found on hillsides in deep shade near black cohosh (*Actaea racemosa*), trillium (*Trillium spp.*), and bloodroot (*Sanguinaria canadensis*).

KEY ACTIONS: Uterine tonic, oxytocic, anti-spasmodic, emmenagogue, anodyne

PART USED: Root

TRADITIONAL USES: Blue cohosh is a valued herb with a long

history of use in the Appalachians. It was used to stimulate and regulate contractions in childbirth and as a general tonic for female reproductive system problems. In addition, blue cohosh was used to relieve joint pain caused by arthritis and rheumatism and as an anti-spasmodic for colic, hiccup, epilepsy, muscle cramps, and spasms.

CURRENT USES: Blue cohosh is a tonic for the female reproductive system. It strengthens uterine function and is often included in formulas to promote fertility, especially for women with a history of miscarriage. Blue cohosh relieves pain caused by endometriosis, fibroid tumors, polycystic ovaries, menses, and menopause. It may bring on delayed menses. During the final weeks of pregnancy, blue cohosh is used as a partus preparator to ensure easy labor. Blue cohosh relieves bronchial spasms and is used in the treatment of asthma, persistent coughs, and bronchitis.

HARVESTING: Dig blue cohosh root in the late summer when the foliage begins to fade. The root and rootlets form a dense, tangled mass that is difficult to unearth and clean.

   Blue cohosh closely resembles meadow rue (*Thalictrum polygamum* or *T. revolutum*). The surface and underside of meadow rue leaves are the same color, unlike blue cohosh, which has a blue-green color on the underside. The flowers of meadow rue are white and give off a distinctive sharp odor when touched. Meadow rue is considered unsafe for internal use.

PREPARATIONS:

   ◊ TINCTURE: Fresh root – 1:2. Menstruum – 75% alcohol. Dried root – 1:5. Menstruum – 50% alcohol.

   ◊ DECOCTION: Use one teaspoon dried or two teaspoons fresh

root for each cup of water. Bring to a boil; cover and simmer for 10 minutes. Strain.

DOSAGES: High doses may cause headaches, nausea, and possibly vomiting. Start with the lowest dose and increase slowly. If necessary, reduce dosage or discontinue. Avoid the use of blue cohosh during the first and second trimesters of pregnancy. Guidance from a practitioner familiar with this herb is strongly recommended before using blue cohosh as a labor tonic.

- TINCTURE: Take 10 to 20 drops, three to four times a day or as needed to relieve symptoms.

- DECOCTION: Drink one cup decoction three to four times a day, or as needed to relieve symptoms.

Boneset

COMMON NAME: Boneset

BOTANICAL NAME: *Eupatorium perfoliatum*

FAMILY: *Asteraceae* (Aster)

OTHER NAMES: Feverwort, ague weed, Indian sage

DESCRIPTION: Boneset is a symmetrical, erect herb, one to four feet tall, with a single stem ending in a slightly branched cluster of small, shaggy, white flowers. It blooms August to October. Boneset has distinctive opposing leaves that are slightly toothed and joined at the base so that the stem appears to puncture the leaves. The leaf has a rough texture and both the leaves and stem are covered with soft white hair.
MPH: p. 89.

HABITAT: Common in sunny open fields, at the edge of forests and along waterways.

KEY ACTIONS: Expectorant, diaphoretic, immune stimulant, antibiotic, digestive bitter, hepatic, analgesic, laxative, emetic

PART USED: Aerial (in flower)

TRADITIONAL USES: Boneset has a long history of use in both

European and American Indian herbal practice. The common name, "boneset," refers to its analgesic properties in treating fever symptoms. Patients given boneset reported that the herb seemed to relieve aching in the bones that accompanied many types of fever.

American Indians used boneset to treat respiratory infections, fevers, poor digestion, and rheumatic pains.

For hundreds of years, boneset was widely used in the treatment of influenza to relieve the body pains that accompanied high fevers. During the 1800s, boneset may have been one of the most frequently used household herbs in the eastern United States. Strong infusions were used to treat fever, colds, coughs, headache, and rheumatism. Boneset was also used as an emetic to remove mucus from the stomach. It was strongly promoted by Eclectic physicians as an immune stimulant and anti-inflammatory agent. Herbalist Tommie Bass of Alabama used boneset in almost every liquid medicine he made. He claimed that many "old-timers" would make a strong, hot boneset infusion and soak their feet in it to "steam themselves."[8] Bass regularly used a cough syrup made with boneset and other herbs.

CURRENT USES: Boneset is one of the most useful herbs for the treatment of colds and influenza. It stimulates immune response, helps reduce fevers and eliminates excess respiratory congestion. As an analgesic, it has a profound effect on body aches and pains caused by fever or rheumatism.

In frequent, small doses, boneset is a digestive system tonic. It has an invigorating effect on the entire digestive process and relieves indigestion, gas, belching, bloating, chronic constipation, and lethargy after eating. It also will improve a poor appetite, especially in the sick and elderly.

HARVESTING: Harvest boneset in late summer just as the flowers begin to bloom. Collect the entire plant from the ground up. If bugs have eaten the lower leaves, cut the stem just above damaged portions.

Boneset dries easily, even in humid weather. Bundle four or five stems together with a rubber band and hang the entire bunch to dry. To keep the herb clean while drying, put the bundled herbs in a paper bag, with the flower end down. Gather the bag around the base of the stems and secure with a second rubber band. The herb is completely dried when leaves crumble easily. Strip leaves and flowers from the stem. Crumble leaves and flowers into small pieces and store in glass jars. Discard the stems.

PREPARATIONS: Due to the bitterness of this herb, consider using it in syrup form. Whenever possible, prepare tinctures and syrups using fresh boneset herb.

◊ TINCTURE: Fresh plant (leaf and flower) – 1:2. Menstruum – 50% alcohol. Dried herb – 1:5. Menstruum – 50% alcohol.

◊ INFUSION: Use one and one-half teaspoons dried or one tablespoon fresh boneset for each cup of water. Steep for 15 minutes. Sweeten liberally with honey to counter the bitter taste.

DOSAGES: Boneset is an intensely bitter herb. This is probably not a remedy to use with children or anyone who is not convinced of the benefits of herbal healing. Boneset tincture and infusion may be used interchangeably. When using boneset infusions to treat respiratory symptoms, add liberal amounts of honey to make the taste bearable. When using boneset as a digestive aid, do not sweeten the tincture or tea; the bitter flavor is central to the medicinal benefits.

Boneset is contraindicated during pregnancy. Doses larger than those recommended here may cause nausea, vomiting, and severe diarrhea. If this occurs, discontinue use.

 # Boneset Syrup

This basic syrup recipe can be made with other herbs, or a combination of herbs, to treat colds, coughs and respiratory infections. Other herbs to consider include maidenhair fern, mullein leaf, rabbit tobacco, sumac berries and sweet gum leaf.

Make an infusion using one ounce of dried or two ounces fresh boneset (leaf and flower) for every pint of water. Pour boiling water over herbs; cover and steep for eight hours or overnight. Strain out the spent herb and discard. Return infusion to a clean pot with a lid. Bring to a boil; cover and simmer until total volume is reduced by half. While mixture is still warm, combine one part concentrated infusion with one-half part honey. Mix well. Store in the refrigerator.

Take one to two teaspoons as needed. Syrup may also be added to hot tea.

◊ TINCTURE FOR RESPIRATORY CONDITIONS: Take 30 to 40 drops of boneset tincture every hour. Add the boneset tincture to a cup of hot water or tea and drink.

◊ TINCTURE FOR DIGESTION: Take 20 to 30 drops of tincture in a small amount of warm water after meals or as needed. For a tonic effect, take daily after each meal for three to six months.

◊ INFUSION FOR RESPIRATORY CONDITIONS: Use hot boneset infusion to treat cold and influenza symptoms. Drink one-half cup infusion, as hot as you can stand it, every hour. Drink at least five doses a day or as needed to relieve symptoms.

◊ INFUSION FOR DIGESTION: To stimulate digestion or as a tonic to improve digestion, take two tablespoons of warm infusion after meals daily for three to six months or as needed.

Devil's Walking Stick

COMMON NAME: Devil's Walking Stick

BOTANICAL NAME: *Aralia spinosa*

FAMILY: *Araliaceae* (Ginseng)

OTHER NAMES: Hercules' club, angelica tree, toothache tree, Southern prickly ash

DESCRIPTION: Devil's walking stick is a tall, graceful plant, between six and 30 feet tall, with sharp spines along a woody trunk and large compound leaves that are often two to four feet in size. Leaves are composed of twice divided leaflets. The individual leaflets are deep green, smooth, and finely toothed. Tiny white flowers bloom in large umbels between June and August followed by abundant deep purple berries in September and October.
MPH: pp. 267-268.

HABITAT: Found in transition zones at the edge of forests and open sunny areas.

KEY ACTIONS: Anti-rheumatic, circulatory stimulant, anti-inflammatory, emetic (in large doses)

PART USED: Berry, bark

TRADITIONAL USES: The Cherokee used the berries and bark to relieve rheumatic pain. Roasted, pounded roots were used in a decoction to make a very strong emetic.[9]

Primarily a home remedy, devil's walking stick has been used to treat earaches (drops of infused bark oil), and to relieve toothaches (chewing on strips of inner bark or packing the tooth with powdered bark) and to treat rheumatic pain (berries infused in liquor).

CURRENT USES: Although devil's walking stick has a long history of use in folk medicine, it is not available commercially. It is a less potent medicine than prickly ash bark (*Zanthoxylum clava-herculis*), though the actions of both plants are similar.

Tincture or decoction of the bark is used to treat rheumatic and arthritic pain. A simple folk tincture made with the ripe berries infused in brandy or other spirits may be taken, one teaspoonful at a time, for joint pain and inflammation, especially when symptoms are worse in cold, damp weather.

Drops of warm infused bark oil are used to relieve earaches. Tincture is applied topically to the teeth and gums to relieve toothaches.

HARVESTING: Harvest berries in the fall when they are a deep purple color. Collect bark in early spring as soon as the plant can be positively identified, or in the fall after the leaves begin to fade. Use long handled loppers and wear leather gloves. Cut the trunk into one-foot lengths. Working carefully, use hand-held clippers to cut off spikes. Then strip the bark from the trunk, with a sharp knife. Cut bark into long thin strips. Process immediately or dry for future use.

PREPARATIONS: Devil's walking stick tincture is made using either the standard weight-to-volume method or the folk tincture method. Directions for both are provided.

◊ TINCTURE: Fresh bark – 1:2. Dried bark – 1:5. Menstruum – 50% alcohol.

◊ FOLK TINCTURE: A traditional folk tincture is made from ripe berries in the fall. Strip berries from the stem and place in a wide-mouthed quart jar. Use a wooden spoon to crush berries and release their juices. Cover completely with brandy, whiskey, or other liquor. Replace lid and shake well. Store in a cool dark place and shake well once a day for at least two weeks. Strain and store in a glass bottle. Herbalist Tommie Bass recommended using 1 pint of 100 proof whiskey for every 6 ounces of fresh berries.[10]

◊ DECOCTION: Use one ounce of dried bark or one and a half ounces fresh bark for each quart of water. Bring to a boil; cover and simmer for 20 minutes. Strain.

◊ INFUSED OIL: Place strips of fresh or dried bark into a heavy cooking pot. Cover the bottom of the pan with bark strips and then pour in enough olive oil to completely submerge the bark. Place the pan on the stove and slowly heat over a low flame, just until the oil begins to bubble. Lower the heat and watch carefully. When the bark appears to be about to fry (it may crackle), remove from heat and cool completely. Strain and discard bark. Store oil in a glass bottle in the refrigerator.

DOSAGES: Although devil's walking stick enjoys a long history of folk use, it is important to use it cautiously and in recommended doses. In large doses, the berries and bark can cause vomiting.

◊ TINCTURE: Take 30 to 50 drops of standard tincture three times a day. Take one teaspoon folk tincture twice a day to relieve rheumatic pain. For toothaches, the bark tincture may be applied directly to the teeth or gums as needed.

◊ DECOCTION: Drink one cup every few hours or as needed to relieve rheumatic pain.

◊ INFUSED OIL: Put one or two drops of warm oil in the ears to relieve pain. Repeat as needed.

Dogwood

COMMON NAME: Dogwood

BOTANICAL NAME: *Cornus florida*

FAMILY: *Cornaceae* (Dogwood)

DESCRIPTION: Dogwood is a small tree, 15 to 20 feet tall, with opposite, oval leaves. In April, the tree appears to be covered with clouds of white flowers. A closer look reveals that these flowers are really four showy white bracts surrounding a cluster of small, bisexual flowers. The foliage turns a brilliant red in early fall. Scarlet berries remain on the tree after the leaves fall and are an important winter food for birds.
    MPH: pp. 303-305.

HABITAT: Common understory tree in deciduous forests.

KEY ACTIONS: Febrifuge, astringent, sedative

PART USED: Bark (aged one year)

TRADITIONAL USES: Before the invention of aspirin, dogwood bark was a valued remedy for the treatment of fevers. During the Civil War, it was used as a substitute for Peruvian cinchona bark, (which contains quinine) to treat malaria, yellow fever, and dysentery.

The ends of dogwood sticks were chewed to create a simple toothbrush credited with keeping teeth brilliant white.

CURRENT USES: Dogwood has fallen out of common usage in modern herbal practice now that malaria, yellow fever, and other dangerous fevers are no longer major health concerns in North America. There is still some folk use of the bark tea for diarrhea.

HARVESTING: Dogwood bark may be harvested throughout the year. Cut several branches from each tree and remove the outer bark in strips using a sharp knife. Chop or cut bark into small pieces. Bark must be dried or cured at least one year before it is safe to use.

PREPARATIONS: Use dried bark that has been aged at least one year.

◊ DECOCTION: Use one tablespoon of thoroughly dried, chopped bark for every pint of water. Bring to a boil; cover and simmer for 15 minutes. Strain.

DOSAGES:

◊ DECOCTION: Drink one-half cup decoction three to four times a day to relieve fevers or diarrhea.

Elder

COMMON NAME: Elder

BOTANICAL NAME: *Sambucus canadensis*

FAMILY: *Caprifoliaceae* (Honeysuckle)

OTHER COMMON NAMES: Elderberry

DESCRIPTION: Elder is a beautiful shrub that grows up to 15 feet tall and has dark green compound leaves with sharply toothed edges. Clusters of small, fragrant white flowers bloom in early summer. In late summer, lush bunches of dark blue-purple berries weigh down the branches. Avoid the toxic (though less common) red elder (*Sambucus pubens*), which has red berries and a black center or pith within the branches.
  MPH: pp. 269-270.

HABITAT: Common around ponds and along streams and found in transition zones at the edge of forests and open sunny areas.

KEY ACTIONS: The entire elder bush is medicinal, but individual actions vary significantly for each part.

  ◊ FLOWER: diaphoretic, expectorant, anti-catarrhal, astringent

  ◊ LEAF: emollient, vulnerary (external use only)

❦ BERRY: anti-viral, diaphoretic, anti-catarrhal, expectorant, laxative, diuretic, astringent

❦ BARK: emetic, cathartic, astringent, anti-inflammatory

PART USED: Flower, leaf, berry, bark

TRADITIONAL USES: Elder is a virtual medicine chest, with a long history of use in both North America and Europe. American Indians used elder flowers to make a pleasant infused beverage. Hot infusions of fresh or dried flowers were used to induce sweating in the treatment of coughs, colds and fevers. An emetic was made from the bark by scraping it off the branches in an upward direction, while bark removed using a downward scraping motion was used as a cathartic. Poultices of leaf and bark were used to treat breast inflammation, burns, wounds, and swellings. Leaves and bark were also combined in salves to treat skin infections, boils, and other hot skin eruptive conditions.[11]

Elderberries are used to make jam, jelly, pie, and wine.

CURRENT USES: Although all parts of the elder shrub have medicinal properties, the flower and berry are most commonly used in herbal practice. Leaf preparations are for external use only. Bark is rarely used. Hot infusions of elder flower are diaphoretic, expectorant, and decongestant; they are commonly used to treat colds and influenza. Taken at the onset of cold and influenza symptoms, elder flower supports the immune response. Elder flower also relieves itchy eyes, runny nose, and throat irritation due to allergies.

The medicinal properties of tart, sweet elderberries are similar to those of the flower, but the berries are also anti-viral. Elderberry syrup soothes coughs, helps treat respiratory infection and relieves allergic reactions. The wonderful flavor of elderberry syrup makes it an excellent remedy for children. Elderberry wine is a gentle digestive aide and is mildly laxative.

Infused elder leaves are used topically as a wash for wounds and burns. Salve made with infused elder leaf oil is used to heal wounds and relieve skin irritations. A fresh leaf poultice helps to relieve painful bruises.

HARVESTING: Elder leaves should be harvested in late spring or early summer, before the flower blooms. Fresh leaves should be allowed to wilt overnight before infusing them in oil to make skin salves.

Elder bark is harvested in the early spring just as the leaves are emerging or in the late fall after berries are gone. The bark is scraped off the larger branches, and smaller, thinner branches may be cut into small pieces and used whole.

Harvest the entire flower cluster when in full bloom at mid-summer. To dry, place each elder flower face down on a screen lined with a thin cotton cloth or a paper towel (in order to catch the pollen and smaller petals that will drop off in the drying process). When the elder flowers are completely dry, store them carefully in glass jars.

Collect berries in late summer. Only ripe berries that are slightly soft and tart should be used. The berries may be frozen, dried or used fresh to make syrup, wine, cordial, jam, or pie.

PREPARATIONS: The most common elder preparations are flower infusions or tinctures, leaf salves, and berry syrups or tinctures.

- TINCTURE OF FLOWERS: Fresh flower – 1:2. Dried flower – 1:5. Menstruum – 50% alcohol.

- TINCTURE OF BERRIES: Fresh berry – 1:2. Dried berry – 1:5. Menstruum – 50% alcohol.

 # Elder Rob Syrup

Elder Rob is a traditional European remedy for treating symptoms of colds and influenza. It also acts as a sleep aid.

Combine five cups of fresh ripe elderberries (stripped from the stalk) with five tablespoons of water in a sturdy pot. Use a wooden spoon to crush the berries. Slowly heat the berries, stirring frequently, until they begin to simmer. Simmer for 30 to 40 minutes. Pour warm mixture through a colander lined with a layer of cheesecloth into a large bowl. Squeeze all the juice from the berries. Measure strained juice into a clean pot; add half as much honey as juice. Bring mixture to a low boil; cook for 10 minutes. Cool and pour into sterile glass jars, cap, label and store in the refrigerator.

Drink two tablespoons of Elder Rob in a cup of hot tea or water as needed.

- ❦ INFUSION: Use two teaspoons dried or one tablespoon fresh flowers (approximately one flower head) for each cup of boiled water. Cover and steep for 20 minutes. Strain. For the strongest diaphoretic effect, reheat before drinking. Sweeten with honey if desired.

- ❦ SYRUP: Make elderberry syrup using the Elder Rob Syrup recipe.

- ❦ SALVE: Make a standard salve using infused elder leaf oil.

DOSAGES:

- ❦ TINCTURE: Take one-half teaspoon of elder flower or berry tincture every hour or as needed to relieve cold and influenza symptoms. To increase diaphoretic properties, add tincture to hot tea before drinking.

- ❦ INFUSION: Drink one cup of hot elder flower infusion every hour or as needed to relieve cold and influenza symptoms such as chest congestion, cough and fever.

- ❦ SALVE: Apply elder leaf salve as needed.

Evening Primrose

COMMON NAME: Evening Primrose

BOTANICAL NAME: *Oenothera biennis*

FAMILY: *Onagraceae* (Evening Primrose)

OTHER NAMES: Sundrops

RELATED SPECIES: *O. fruticosa, O. lacinata, O. perennis*

DESCRIPTION: Evening primrose is an herbaceous biennial, one to three feet tall. Leaves are lance-shaped with a rough surface and slightly ragged edges that are tinged with red. In the first year, leaves form a basal cluster. In the second, the flower stalk emerges. Fragrant yellow blooms appear July to September with four sepals and petals, four or eight stamens, and a conspicuous four-lobed stigma that forms a cross. Blossoms first open at dusk in mid-summer, stay open for one night and fade by dawn. During the shorter days of late summer, flowers remain open into daylight hours. Flowers are pollinated by rosy maple moths (*Dryocampa rubicunda*).

Other species, such as *O. fruticosa* and *O. perennis*, bloom in the morning.

MPH: pp. 106-107.

HABITAT: Common along roadsides, in fields and open sunny

areas, evening primrose tolerates dry, poor soil conditions. Plants are scattered widely and are difficult to identify until they flower.

KEY ACTIONS: Demulcent, emollient, nervine, anti-spasmodic

PART USED: Entire plant (root, leaf, flower)

TRADITIONAL USES: Evening primrose is indigenous to both North America and Europe, where it has a long history of use as a medicine and as a food. Poultices of the fresh root were used by American Indians to treat wounds, sores, hemorrhoids, and other inflammatory conditions.[12]

Evening primrose has been used as a folk remedy for a wide range of symptoms such as sore throat, cough, upset stomach, urinary tract infection, and skin problems. In Southern folk medicine, evening primrose tea is a remedy for nervousness and hysteria.

Spring-harvested leaves, roots collected from the first-year plants, and seeds have been used as wild foods.

CURRENT USES: Evening primrose is a mild remedy used as a relaxing nervine and as a demulcent for coughs and sore throats. Aerial parts of the plant are used in salves and poultices to treat inflammation, infection, itching, and other hot eruptive skin conditions.

Oil extracted from the seed is an important nutritional supplement and source of omega-6 oils. Research has shown that the oil of evening primrose seed contains two important essential fatty acids: gamma-linolenic (GLA) and linoleic acid (LA). These fatty acids play a role in the treatment of pre-menstrual syndrome, eczema, psoriasis, high cholesterol, arthritis, migraines, and asthma. Research also indicates that in high doses (five to eight grams a day) evening primrose oil may help to relieve symptoms of

Attention Deficit Disorder and Attention Deficit/Hyperactivity Disorder.[13]

HARVESTING: Harvest evening primrose when it is in flower in early summer. Gather the entire plant, including the roots. Rinse away any dirt and dry completely. Leaves harvested in early spring and roots of plants in their first year of growth (before the flower stalk appears) are edible.

PREPARATIONS:

◊ INFUSION: Use one generous handful of fresh evening primrose herb (leaf, flower, root and stem) for each pint of water. Cover and steep for 10 minutes. Strain. Sweeten with honey.

◊ SYRUP: To make a simple cough syrup,[14] finely chop four or five evening primrose plants and mix with twice as much honey. Bring to a gentle boil and cook for 20 minutes. Cool and strain. Store in the refrigerator.

◊ SALVE: Make a standard salve with infused evening primrose oil.

DOSAGES:

◊ INFUSION: Drink one cup of evening primrose infusion two to three times a day or as needed. Evening primrose may be combined with other nervines like black cohosh (*Actaea racemosa*) and skullcap (*Scutellaria lateriflora*).

◊ SYRUP: Take one tablespoon of evening primrose syrup every half-hour or as needed to relieve coughs and soothe throat irritation.

◊ SALVE: Use a fresh herb salve as needed.

Evening Primrose Poultice

A poultice made of fresh herbs is an effective treatment for skin rashes, infections, wounds, ulcers, or burns and usually speeds up healing.

This general recipe may be used with any number of skin herbs, alone or in a combination of your choice. Other herbs to consider include elder leaves, goldenrod, jewelweed and passionflower leaves.

Gather and clean fresh plants. Chop finely and crush or pound using a mortar and pestle. The crushed herbs should produce enough juices to hold them together. If necessary, add a small amount of aloe vera gel, water or honey and mix well until herbs form a mass.

Apply poultice directly to the skin. Cover with a piece of gauze or cotton cloth. Leave poultice in place for 20 minutes. Remove poultice and discard herbs. Repeat as often as needed.

Fringetree

COMMON NAME: Fringetree

BOTANICAL NAME: *Chionanthus virginica*

FAMILY: *Oleaceae* (Olive)

OTHER NAMES: White ash, Grancy Gray Beard, granddad's beard

DESCRIPTION: Fringetree is a small tree, four to 20 feet tall, with smooth oval leaves. Distinctive white flowers have long, narrow, fringe-like petals that grow in drooping arches. Blooms appear in May and June. The fruit resembles a small blue-black olive.
   MPH: pp. 303-304.

HABITAT: Deciduous hardwood forests.

KEY ACTIONS: Hepatic, cholagogue, diuretic, alterative, anti-inflammatory

PART USED: Dried root bark

TRADITIONAL USES: American Indians used the bark and root as a wash or poultice to treat bruises, cuts, and infected wounds.[15] In Southern folk medicine, fringetree was used to reduce fevers, improve liver function, and restore the appetite after an illness.[16]

Fringetree - Chionanthus virginica

In the 19th century, Eclectic physicians praised fringetree as one of the most valuable remedies for liver disease. Considered a cure for jaundice, it was also used to treat gallstones, kidney stones, liver weakness, and pelvic congestion.[17]

CURRENT USES: Fringetree is still an important remedy for the treatment of liver problems. It is used to improve liver function and stimulate bile secretions and also is a specific remedy to treat jaundice, gallbladder inflammation, and gallstones. As a tonic, fringetree helps to prevent the formation of gallstones. Regular use improves digestion and elimination, and stimulates the appetite. Fringetree is an excellent liver tonic for anyone with a history of excessive drug or alcohol use. Use the decoction to clean wounds or as a compress on bruises.

HARVESTING: Harvest root bark in early spring just as leaves emerge, or in the fall as the first frost approaches. To locate surface roots, dig straight down starting beneath the drip line of the tree (directly below the outermost tips of the leaves, or just beyond outer branches of smaller trees). Immediately after harvesting, wash the root and peel off the outer bark. Cut into small pieces and dry completely before using.

PREPARATIONS:

◖ TINCTURE: Dried root bark – 1:5. Menstruum – 60% alcohol.

◖ DECOCTION: Use two teaspoons of dried root bark for each cup of water. Bring to a boil; cover and simmer for 20 minutes. Strain.

DOSAGES:

◖ TINCTURE: For acute symptoms, take 10 to 20 drops in a small

amount of water every 30 minutes to two hours until symptoms improve. To improve digestion, take 20 drops after
meals. As a general tonic for the liver, take 10 to 20 drops
three times a day, preferably after meals.

⧫ DECOCTION: Use decoction as a wash to clean skin infections
or as hot compress on painful bruises.

Gentian

COMMON NAME: Gentian

BOTANICAL NAME: *Gentiana quinquefolia*

FAMILY: *Gentianaceae* (Gentian)

OTHER NAMES: Ague-weed, stiff gentian

RELATED SPECIES: Blue gentian (*G. villosa* or *G. catesbaei*), striped gentian (*G. decora*), fringed gentian (*G. crinita*), and closed or bottle gentian (*G. clausa*) are also found in the region. European gentian (*G. lutea*) is used interchangeably with *G. quinquefolia*.

DESCRIPTION: Gentian is an annual herb, one to two feet tall, with narrow oval leaves in pairs. Branched stems have five or more flowers in clusters at the terminal end. The small, three-fourth inch upright, tubular flowers vary in color from deep purple to pale blue and appear between July and October. The flower petals remain tightly closed until opened by a pollinator.
  MPH: p. 200.

HABITAT: Grows along stream banks and ponds, in transition zones along the edge of forests and in open sunny areas.

KEY ACTIONS: Bitter, hepatic, stomachic, sialogogue, digestive tonic, laxative, emmenagogue

PART USED: Root

TRADITIONAL USES: In Europe, gentian is a traditional digestive bitter used to stimulate digestion, especially after a rich meal. A gentian root along with other bitter herbs was often steeped in brandy or other liquor to make a simple digestive bitter. The root was chewed to numb the gums.

    King's American Dispensatory, first published in 1893, recommended gentian "where the powers of life are depressed and recovery depends on the ability to assimilate food." Gentian was also recommended as a specific remedy for headaches, liver problems, jaundice, weak digestion, and gallbladder problems.[18]

CURRENT USES: Gentian is used to treat chronic digestive problems with symptoms of bloating, gas, belching, constipation, and headaches. Used regularly as a digestive bitter, gentian improves digestion, assimilation, and elimination. It stimulates the appetite and is considered a general tonic for those suffering from weakness and fatigue, especially when digestion and appetite are poor.

HARVESTING: Collect the root in the late summer or fall as the flowers begin to fade.

PREPARATIONS: Gentian root is often combined with other warming aromatic herbs (such as orange peel, ginger, cinnamon, fennel, and cardamom) to mask its bitter flavor and increase its effectiveness.

Gentian Digestive Bitters

A small dose of bitters after a meal helps improve digestion.

Put three ounces of ground dry or five ounces of finely chopped, fresh gentian root into a quart jar with the skins of two organic oranges (thinly sliced), one tablespoon of ground cardamom seed, one teaspoon whole fennel seed and 16 ounces of quality brandy. Replace lid and shake well. Store in a cool place for one month, shaking well every few days.

After one month, strain out the spent herbs and discard. Add one-fourth cup honey and mix well. Store in a glass bottle.

Take one to two teaspoons in a small amount of warm water or tea after meals. For an energizing drink, add one tablespoon of bitters to one cup of sparkling mineral water.

◊ TINCTURE: Fresh root – 1:2. Dried root – 1:5. Menstruum – 50% alcohol.

DOSAGES: In large doses, gentian tincture can irritate the stomach and cause nausea, or even vomiting and diarrhea. At the correct dose, gentian relieves gastric inflammation and other digestive upsets. Always start with a low dose and increase gradually if needed. Gentian should not be used by anyone with a stomach ulcer or severe nausea.

◊ TINCTURE: Take 10 to 20 drops in a small amount of warm water after meals or as needed. As a tonic, take 10 to 20 drops three times a day for a month or longer.

Ginseng

COMMON NAME: Ginseng

BOTANICAL NAME: *Panax quinquefolius*

FAMILY: *Araliaceae* (Ginseng)

OTHER NAMES: American ginseng, sang

RELATED SPECIES: Dwarf ginseng (*Panax trifolius*), Asian or Korean ginseng (*Panax ginseng*)

DESCRIPTION: Ginseng is a low-growing perennial, six to eight inches tall, found in the deep shade of deciduous forests. Each plant has two to four leaves, each on a single stem. Leaves are divided into five sharply toothed leaflets; the center three are larger than the outer two. Tucked at the center of the plant, small inconspicuous green flowers bloom in midsummer. The fruit, a bulging cluster of green berries, turns brilliant red in the fall. Ginseng root is white and fragrant. The roots of young plants form a single carrot-shaped taproot. After several years, the roots branch and are thought to resemble the shape of a small human body.
    MPH: pp. 58-60.

HABITAT: Rich soil of deciduous hardwood forests. American ginseng is often found in plant communities that include bloodroot (*Sanguinaria canadensis*), black cohosh (*Actaea racemosa*) and wild ginger (*Asarum canadense*). Once very common throughout eastern North America, ginseng has been over-harvested for the past three hundred years, and wild stands are now rare. Ginseng is a protected plant throughout the southern Appalachians.

KEY ACTIONS: Adaptogen, tonic, stimulant, carminative, demulcent

PART USED: Root, leaf

TRADITIONAL USES: Ginseng is one of the most prized tonic herbs in eastern Asia where it has been used for thousands of years to promote longevity.[19] In North America, it was used extensively by eastern American Indians to relieve an array of symptoms including general fatigue, headache, palsy, fevers, thrush, rheumatism, breathing difficulties, and colic. It was also used as a good luck charm and was thought to prevent children from having bad dreams.[20]

CURRENT USES: In modern herbal practice, ginseng is still an exalted tonic. American ginseng is considered a cooling herb appropriate for a wide range of symptoms caused by weakness and fatigue. Long-term use is recommended to remedy health problems caused by stress, overwork, poor diet, sleep difficulties, traumatic injuries, and aging.

Ginseng nourishes all body fluids. It is a specific remedy for dry coughs and lung inflammation with fever, weakness, and thirst. Ginseng helps to restore flexibility in the ligaments and tendons, moisten the skin and mucus membranes, and nourish the blood. By increasing fluids throughout the body, ginseng has a calming effect that improves concentration, sleep quality, digestion, and elimination. Long-term use harmonizes the function of all the organs.

Clinical studies have shown that ginseng improves eye/hand coordination and increases concentration, alertness, and the ability to grasp abstract concepts.[21]

HARVESTING: In all states where it grows wild, the collection of wild ginseng roots requires a permit, and sale is regulated by state and federal laws. For personal use, ginseng may be grown in the right conditions from roots or seeds. Harvest three-to six-year-old roots when the ginseng berry turns brilliant red in the fall. Fresh roots can be sliced into small pieces or dried whole if they are small (less than six inches long.) To propagate a new plant after digging out the root, plant the ripe berry in the hole about one inch below the surface. Cover with dirt.

PREPARATIONS: The root of ginseng is the primary part of the plant used. The leaf is also used as a tea, although it is considered a weaker medicine. Ginseng roots may also be used as an ingredient in soup stock, especially during the winter or when preparing meals for anyone recovering from illness.

◊ TINCTURES: Fresh root – 1:2. Dried root – 1:5. Menstruum – 45% to 60% alcohol.

◊ DECOCTION: Use one tablespoon dried, chopped root or one small whole root (about two to three inches long) for every 12 ounces of water. Small roots may be used whole. Bring to a boil; cover and simmer until the liquid is reduced to about eight ounces. Strain. Use each ginseng root three or four times before discarding. Store roots in the refrigerator between decoctions.

DOSAGES: To be an effective tonic, American ginseng requires long-term use. At least three to six months of daily use is recommended for most conditions described above. Ginseng is an excellent seasonal tonic for the winter months. Although side effects are rare, if heart palpitations, headaches, insomnia or elevated blood pressure occur, reduce dosage or discontinue use.

◊ TINCTURE: Take 20 to 40 drops three times a day.

◊ DECOCTION: Drink one or more cups three times a day.

Goldenrod

COMMON NAME: Goldenrod

BOTANICAL NAME: *Solidago spp.*

FAMILY: *Asteraceae* (Aster)

OTHER NAMES: Farewell-to-summer, Aaron's rod, woundwort, sweet goldenrod, anise-scented goldenrod

RELATED SPECIES: The two species of goldenrod with the most documented use in the region are *S. odora* (sweet or anise-scented goldenrod) and *S. canadensis* (Canadian goldenrod). There are more than 38 species of goldenrod growing in the Appalachians, and positive identification is difficult even for the most exacting botanist. Fortunately, the medicinal properties of most species are similar.

DESCRIPTION: Goldenrod is an erect perennial, two to five feet tall, with a solitary stem, sometimes branched or arching. Lance-shaped leaves are two to three inches long with a rough surface texture. Leaf margins vary according to species; *S. odora* has smooth edges while *S. canadensis* is toothed.

Small, ragged golden-yellow flowers grow in terminal plumes and bloom from late summer until frost. *S. odora* flowers grow to one side of the stalk; the leaves when crushed smell like anise. The flowers of *S. canadensis* form a triangular plume.

MPH: pp. 139-140.

HABITAT: Dry, open sunny areas.

KEY ACTIONS: Anti-catarrhal, astringent, diaphoretic, vulnerary, anti-lithic, sedative

PART USED: Aerial (in flower)

TRADITIONAL USES: American Indians used goldenrod as a soothing remedy for diarrhea, to reduce fevers, relieve coughs, and as a general sedative. They bandaged wounds and burns with fresh goldenrod leaves and applied fresh leaf poultices to the head to relieve headaches. Infusions of goldenrod were added to baths to relax women during labor and to calm fussy babies.[22]

In the early years of the 19th century, goldenrod tea was promoted as a popular beverage in the eastern United States. It was known as Blue Mountain Tea in the southern Appalachians, where it was considered a remedy for exhaustion and fatigue.[23]

In Europe, the goldenrod species *S. virgauria* is used to treat urinary infections, to dissolve or eliminate kidney stones, and to reduce inflammation and congestion in the upper respiratory system.

CURRENT USES: Goldenrod is an underused herb in modern herbal practice. It is an effective remedy for upper respiratory inflammation and congestion. Use goldenrod to treat rhinitis, seasonal allergy, sinus infection, cold and influenza. The infusion is used as a gargle for laryngitis and sore throats.

As an anti-inflammatory, goldenrod is used as a tea for heartburn, indigestion, and diarrhea. It also relieves inflammation caused by bladder infections and may prevent or dissolve kidney stones.

In salves, goldenrod promotes the healing of ulcers, wounds, and burns.

HARVESTING: Gather goldenrod as it begins to bloom in mid to late summer. Because the leaves are covered with fine hair, try to harvest on a clear day immediately after a good rainfall has cleaned the plant of dirt and debris. Cut the stem above any dirty or bug-eaten leaves.

If using the fresh herb, strip leaves and flowers from the stem and prepare immediately.

To dry, bundle four or five goldenrod stems together, using a rubber band, and hang in a well-ventilated area; or strip the leaves and flowers from the stalk and spread evenly on a screen. Goldenrod dries easily, although you may have to break up the flower clusters to keep them from molding.

PREPARATIONS: Goldenrod makes a delicious tea. When using bitter or harsh herbs, adding some goldenrod to the blend improves the flavor of the tea.

- TINCTURE: Fresh herb – 1:2. Dry herb – 1:5. Menstruum – 35 to 50% alcohol.

- INFUSION: Use one tablespoon dried or two tablespoons fresh herb for each cup of water. Cover and steep for 20 minutes. Strain.

- SALVE: Prepare a standard salve using infused goldenrod oil.

- POULTICE: Poultice fresh leaves by pounding them with a mortar and pestle to make a paste. Add water or aloe vera gel as needed to hold leaves together. Apply to wounds or burns to reduce inflammation and to promote healing.

DOSAGES:

◊ TINCTURE: Take 20 to 40 drops three times a day or as needed. For best results, add the tincture to hot tea. Take 40 drops tincture twice a day as a tonic for kidney stones.

◊ INFUSION: Drink one cup hot infusion every one to two hours, or as needed. Drink two to three cups a day as a tonic for kidney stones.

◊ SALVE: Apply as needed to the skin.

◊ POULTICE: Apply fresh leaf poultice to burns, wounds, and other skin inflammations. Remove poultice after about 10 minutes, or sooner if the poultice gets hot. Repeat as often as needed.

Indian Pipe

COMMON NAME: Indian Pipe

BOTANICAL NAME: *Monotropa uniflora*

FAMILY: *Ericaceae* (Heath)

OTHER NAMES: Ghost flower, corpse plant, ice plant

DESCRIPTION: Indian pipe is a distinctive white, semi-transparent perennial. A saprophytic plant that contains no chlorophyll, Indian pipe is unable to process sunlight. For nutrients, it relies on a symbiotic relationship with molds and other fungi found in the decaying leaf humus at the base of trees. This small plant, only four to six inches tall, consists of a scaled, tube-like stalk that ends in a nodding, solitary white flower. It grows in clumps and looks like a cluster of small white pipes with their stems stuck into the ground. As the flower blooms between June and September, Indian pipe slowly straightens into an upright position with the flower pointed eventually towards the sky.

The flowers have no fragrance. After pollination or if disturbed, Indian pipe turns black and dissolves.

MPH: pp. 32-33.

HABITAT: Deeply shaded moist woodlands, usually in acid soil beneath rhododendron and mountain laurel.

KEY ACTIONS: Anodyne, anti-spasmodic, sedative, diaphoretic

PART USED: Entire plant

TRADITIONAL USES: This plant was well known to the Cherokee as a pain remedy of the highest order, comparable to morphine. They also used Indian pipe for *petit mal* seizures, Bell's palsy, nervous tics, and convulsions caused by fevers. Juice of the fresh plant, combined with saltwater, was used for inflammation of the eyes.[24]

CURRENT USES: Use of Indian pipe is limited due to the fragile nature of the plant itself and the lack of commercial sources.

Indian pipe dulls the perception of pain without causing drowsiness. To relieve specific types of pain, it is paired with anti-inflammatories such as willow (*Salix spp.*), or anti-spasmodics such as wild yam (*Dioscorea villosa*), black cohosh (*Actaea racemosa*) and black haw (*Viburnum prunifolium*).

HARVESTING: There are no known methods for cultivating Indian pipe; all plants are gathered from the wild. Because its native habitat is dwindling, the use of Indian pipe is limited to small-scale use by individuals with access to sites where it grows.

Indian pipe seems to magically appear fully formed in the cool darkness of rhododendron thickets. After a day or two, its flowers are pollinated and begin to decay. As soon as it emerges, harvest the entire plant including the root. The flowers should be curved over, facing the ground. As the plant matures, the flower stalks slowly straighten until the flowers are facing upright. Within hours they begin to fade. It is too late to harvest Indian pipe if the flowers are upright, or in full bloom, and their edges have begun to blacken. An extremely fragile plant, it must be processed immediately. Even a gentle touch can cause bruising. It is a good idea to bring prepared menstruum and jars with you into the forest so you can make the tincture immediately after harvesting. You will also need a small brush, water, and a bowl to clean the roots.

PREPARATIONS: Indian pipe is best used in tincture form. The tincture has a beautiful violet color.

◊ TINCTURE: Fresh plant – 1:2. Menstruum – 35% alcohol.

DOSAGES: Experiment with dosage to find one that relieves pain symptoms. Frequent small doses seem to work best. Once the pain cycle has been disrupted, it may be possible to reduce the dosage frequency needed to manage symptoms. Not recommended for long term use (more than one month of daily use).

◊ TINCTURE: Start with 40 drops every half-hour. If pain is not diminished after three or four doses, increase to 50 drops. Increase dosage amount as needed to manage symptoms. For severe pain, doses as high as one tablespoon per hour may be needed. Once pain level improves, increase the amount of time between doses and reduce the dosage amount to control symptoms.

Jewelweed

COMMON NAME: Jewelweed

BOTANICAL NAME: *Impatiens capensis*

FAMILY: *Balsaminaceae* (Touch-Me-Not)

OTHER NAMES: Touch-me-not, spotted touch-me-not

RELATED SPECIES: Yellow jewelweed or pale touch-me-not (*Impatiens pallida*)

DESCRIPTION: Jewelweed is a succulent annual that grows two to four feet tall. The entire plant is smooth and slightly translucent. Leaves are oval, with scalloped edges; they grow in pairs in the lower parts of the plant and then singly along the stem towards the top. When the leaves or stems are crushed, they secrete a gel-like substance.

Flowers hang like pendants on short arched stems beneath the leaves. They are irregular, with five petals: the upper two are united; the lower three separate with a long spur at the back. *I. capensis* has orange flowers with tiny red dots, while *I. pallida* has yellow flowers and a shorter spur. Both species have the same medicinal properties. Jewelweed blooms from July to September.

Jewelweed gets its name from how beads of rain or dew on its leaves glitter like diamonds. Its other common name is, "touch-me-not," which describes how the ripe seed pods explode when touched, flinging the seeds far from the plant.

MPH: *I. capensis* pp. 154-155; *I. pallida* p. 120.

HABITAT: Abundant in cool, wet places throughout the region. According to folklore, jewelweed is always found growing near poison ivy.

KEY ACTIONS: Astringent, anti-inflammatory, emollient

PART USED: Aerial (when in flower)

TRADITIONAL USES: The Cherokee used jewelweed juice to soothe poison ivy rash. The crushed leaves were rubbed on children's bellies to relieve a sour stomach. An infusion was used in a bath for women in the final stages of pregnancy. The plant was also used ceremonially.[25]

CURRENT USES: Jewelweed retains its exalted place as one of the most effective remedies to relieve skin inflammation, rash, and itching caused by poison ivy. Poultices, salves and frozen infusion ice cubes (see recipe) are used to treat poison ivy, skin rashes, insect bites, abrasions, and other skin irritations. Young plants are cooked as a potherb in the early spring. Fresh jewelweed leaves are rubbed on the skin to prevent a reaction to poison ivy.

HARVESTING: Gather jewelweed anytime during the growing season. However, like many plants, it loses vigor as summer wanes and should be harvested during June or July. Jewelweed grows in large masses, making it possible to harvest many plants with very little effort. The root easily comes out of the ground, and you may harvest large quantities of jewelweed by pulling them up in bunches. If you use this method, cut off the roots immediately so they

Jewelweed Infusion Ice Cubes

When treating poison ivy rash or insect bites, soothing, anti-inflammatory jewelweed in combination with the numbing effect of ice is pure heaven. Make up a big batch of ice cubes early each summer and keep them in the freezer to have on hand when needed.

Gather eight or nine fresh jewelweed plants. Rinse gently to clean. Chop coarsely and place in a blender or food processor. Add enough water to completely submerge the plants. Process until smooth. Pour into a quart-size canning jar, cover and steep for six hours or overnight. Pour infusion into ice-cube trays and freeze. Alternately, if working without a food processor or blender, strain the infusion after it is ready, discard herbs and freeze the infusion as above.

Gently rub jewelweed ice cubes on irritated, itchy skin as often as need.

don't get the aerial parts dirty. If using the more precise method, cut each plant near the ground. Once harvested, jewelweed wilts quickly and shrivels to almost half its original size. Consequently, large amounts are needed.

PREPARATIONS: Jewelweed is used externally for the treatment of skin inflammation and irritation.

⬧ POULTICE: Put five or six fresh jewelweed plants in a blender or food processor with one-fourth to one-half cup aloe vera gel. Blend until mixture is smooth. Add eight to 10 drops of lavender essential oil. Blend once more. Use immediately or pour into a wide mouthed jar and refrigerate. Apply liberally as needed to poison ivy rash or other inflamed itchy skin conditions.

⬧ SALVE: Allow fresh jewelweed to wilt for several hours or overnight before making infused oil for salve.

DOSAGES: Use jewelweed preparations described here as often as needed to relieve itching and inflammation of the skin.

Joe-pye-weed

COMMON NAME: Joe-pye-weed

BOTANICAL NAME: *Eupatorium purpureum*

FAMILY: *Asteraceae* (Aster)

OTHER NAMES: Gravel root, sweet Joe-pye-weed, Queen of the Meadow, purple boneset

RELATED SPECIES: *E. maculatum* (spotted Joe-pye-weed), *E. fistulosum*, *E. serotinum*

DESCRIPTION: Joe-pye-weed is a dramatic plant, sometimes reaching heights of 10 to 14 feet, with a single stalk crowned by a royal plume of purple flowers. Lance-shaped leaves with serrated edges and a rough surface texture grow in whorls of four or six leaves around the stem. In late summer, flowers appear in ragged clumps at the top of the plant. The stalk is hollow.

To differentiate between the two most common species of Joe-pye-weed found in the region, note that the flowers of *E. purpureum* form a mounded tuft; the leaves are aromatic, and dark purple marks appear at the leaf nodes. Conversely, the flowers of *E. maculatum* form a flat-topped cluster; there are purple spots along the stem, and it is only three to four feet in height.

MPH: pp. 185-186.

HABITAT: Joe-pye-weed likes full sun and wet feet. It is found in sunny open areas along ditches, ponds and lakes. Common companion plants found growing near Joe-pye-weed include boneset (*Eupatorium perfoliatum*), jewelweed (*Impatiens capensis, I. pallida*), and elder (*Sambucus canadensis*).

KEY ACTIONS:

♦ LEAF: Diaphoretic, analgesic

♦ ROOT: Diuretic, anti-lithic, kidney tonic, anti-inflammatory, astringent, anti-rheumatic

PART USED: Leaf or root

TRADITIONAL USES: There are several legends about the origin of the common name. One asserts that Joe Pye was a so-called "Indian theme promoter," who marketed an extract of the plant as a cure for typhoid fever.[26] Another source claims that the name derives from "jopi," the word for typhoid fever in an American Indian language.[27]

The Cherokee used the hollow tubes of the plant's stem through which to "bubble" or blow air into herbal medicines to activate them and increase their potency.[28] The stems were also used to blow herbal remedies on and around the person to be healed.

Herbalist Tommie Bass used the root to treat kidney and bladder disease, prostate problems and kidney stones. He claimed that the root had a balancing effect on blood sugar levels and used it in the treatment of type II (non-insulin dependent) diabetes. Bass also recommended Joe-pye-weed for the relief of rheumatic pain.[29]

CURRENT USES: Joe-pye-weed root is one of the best restoratives to treat chronic diseases of the urinary tract. It is a specific remedy for the treatment of prostate inflammation and swelling, cystitis, urinary tract infections and urgent or frequent urination. Joe-pye-weed may help to prevent the formation of kidney stones. It also relieves the pain and discomfort associated with bladder infections, prostatitis, and interstitial cystitis. The diuretic action of the root helps to relieve joint pain and inflammation caused by rheumatic conditions.

Joe-pye-weed leaves reduce fevers and the body aches that often accompany colds and influenza. As a diaphoretic, the action is similar to boneset (*Eupatorium perfoliatum*).

HARVESTING: Collect the leaves just as the flowers begin to bloom in mid to late summer. Bundle the stems together and hang in a cool dark place until completely dry. Strip the dry leaves and flowers from the stem and store in glass jars. Leaves may also be stripped from the stems and dried on screens or in a dehydrator.

Joe-pye-weed roots are best harvested as the flowers being to fade in late summer or early fall. Clean the roots completely and chop into small pieces. To dry, spread on a screen and turn frequently or place in a dehydrator until completely dry.

PREPARATIONS: Joe-pye-weed is an intensely bitter herb. Sweeten tea preparations with liberal amounts of honey or add tincture to fruit juice.

- TINCTURE: Fresh leaf or root – 1:2. Dried leaf or root – 1:5. Menstruum – 50% alcohol.

- INFUSION: Use one teaspoon dried or two teaspoons fresh leaf for each cup of water. Cover and infuse for 20 minutes. Strain and sweeten with honey.

- DECOCTION: Use one teaspoon dried or two teaspoons fresh

root for each cup of water. Bring to a boil; cover and simmer for 10 minutes. Strain and sweeten with honey.

DOSAGES: Joe-pye-weed is contraindicated during pregnancy.

◊ TINCTURE: For acute symptoms, take 10 to 20 drops leaf or root tincture in a small amount of water or juice every half hour until symptoms improve. For chronic kidney problems, take 20 drops root tincture twice a day in a small amount of water for one month or longer.

◊ INFUSION: Drink one cup of hot leaf infusion every hour to reduce fever or relieve rheumatic pain.

◊ DECOCTION: Drink one cup of cool or slightly warm root decoction every half-hour to relieve acute urinary tract discomfort. As a tonic for chronic kidney problems, drink two to three cups of warm decoction each day for several months.

Lobelia

COMMON NAME: Lobelia

BOTANICAL NAME: *Lobelia inflata*

FAMILY: *Campanulaceae* (Harebell)

OTHER NAMES: Indian tobacco, pukeweed, vomitwort, asthma weed

RELATED SPECIES: *L. spicata var. scaposa, L. siphilitica, L. cardinalis*

DESCRIPTION: Lobelia is an erect annual, one to two feet tall. The alternate leaves, one to three inches long, are smooth with a deep green color. Tiny pale blue flowers, one-fourth inch in size, emerge at an angle between the leaf and the stem. Lobelia blooms appear July to September. The plant derives its species name from the appearance of the seedpods that swell up, or "inflate," and turn yellow when ripe.
    MPH: pp. 207-209; *L. cardinalis*, pp. 163-164.

HABITAT: Lobelia is found in partial shade along roadways and the edges of fields. It is an inconspicuous plant and is easy to overlook.

KEY ACTIONS: Anti-spasmodic, expectorant, emetic

PART USED: Leaf and flower

TRADITIONAL USES: Lobelia has a notorious past. Although it has had a place in both American Indian and European herbal traditions, its reputation was tarnished when it was implicated in a much publicized murder trial in the 19th century. A naturopathic physician, Samuel Thomson, was accused and later acquitted of killing one of his patients with an overdose of lobelia. Even though there is no evidence in the past two hundred years' medical literature of the plant's ever having caused any adverse effect more serious than vomiting,[30] lobelia's undeserved reputation as a dangerous plant persists.

Cherokees used lobelia in large doses to induce vomiting and in small doses to reduce spasms in cases of colic and croup. It was also used topically to relax muscle spasms and relieve body aches. Lobelia was smoked as a tobacco substitute.[31]

Writing in the mid 1800s, Dr. Frances P. Porcher notes that lobelia is "one of the most valuable of our indigenous plants."[32] He recommended using small doses of the infusion to relieve convulsions, to stop heart palpitations, to induce sweating, and to prevent colic and croup in infants.

CURRENT USES: Lobelia is an important herb used to treat acute respiratory problems. It relieves spasmodic coughs, asthma, and allergy-induced breathing difficulties. For acute symptoms, lobelia acts quickly and effectively as a bronchial dilator and relaxant. Long-term use is not recommended. The herb is smoked to help ease nicotine withdrawal and asthmatic symptoms.

Lobelia tincture is used in small frequent doses to relieve muscle cramps, spasms, and body aches. Tincture or liniment may be applied directly on the skin to relieve these same symptoms.

HARVESTING: Collect the entire plant just as the seeds begin to mature. There should be both flowers and ripe seedpods on the plant. Mature seedpods look like little pale yellow inflated balloons. Once the seeds ripen, the plant quickly fades. Freshly harvested lobelia should be tinctured immediately. Dry lobelia for use in smoking mixtures.

Related species, *L. spicata var. scaposa, L. siphilitica,* and *L. cardinalis,* also have active properties, but *L. inflata* is the traditional species used in herbal practice.

PREPARATIONS: Lobelia tincture is made using the standard weight-to-volume method. A second traditional method of making a simple tincture is also included below.

◊ TINCTURE: Fresh herb – 1:2. Dry herb – 1:5. Menstruum – 75% alcohol.

◊ TRADITIONAL TINCTURE METHOD: Gather lobelia plants at any stage of growth. If they are small, take the roots as well. Crush the fresh herb in a mortar and mix in an equal amount of quality alcohol. Quality brandy is a good choice. When thoroughly blended, carefully strain through a fine piece of muslin fabric, and squeeze out every drop of liquid. Store in a brown bottle.[33]

◊ HERBAL SMOKE INHALATION: Mix dried lobelia with an equal amount of dried mullein (*Verbascum thapsus*) leaf or flower. Crumble all herbs as finely as possible. Put a small amount of mixture in a pipe and light.

DOSAGES: Using lobelia medicinally requires careful attention to dosage. Compared to other medicinal herbs, it is used in very low doses. Small amounts are very effective at relieving spasm, cramps, and breathing difficulties. Large doses cause nausea and

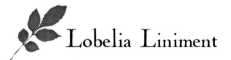 # Lobelia Liniment

When applied directly to the skin over a problem area, lobelia liniment is a fast-acting muscle relaxant.

To make a simple liniment, fill a pint jar half full of crushed, fresh lobelia plants. Cover the herb with rubbing alcohol, rice wine (sake), or apple cider vinegar. Replace the lid and shake briskly. Steep for five days, shaking well several times a day. Strain out spent herb and discard.

Store lobelia liniment in a bottle clearly labeled: For External Use Only.

To use, apply liniment with cotton directly on the skin over muscle spasms and contractions. Apply every 20 minutes or as needed to relieve symptoms.

Liniment keeps for about a year.

even vomiting. Lobelia is contraindicated during pregnancy or for those with heart problems.

◊ TINCTURE: Take 10 to 20 drops in a small amount of water or tea every 30 minutes until symptoms are relieved.

◊ HERBAL SMOKE INHALATION: Take small inhalations of smoke into the lungs, hold for a few seconds and exhale. Repeat two or three times or until breathing becomes easier. Use smoke inhalations sparingly to relieve acute symptoms, because smoke is very drying to the lungs.

Maidenhair Fern

COMMON NAME: Maidenhair Fern

BOTANICAL NAME: *Adiantum pedatum*

FAMILY: *Polypodiaceae* (Fern)

OTHER NAMES: Finger fern, five finger fern, pointer weed

RELATED SPECIES: European maidenhair (*A. capillus-veneris*) has the same actions.

DESCRIPTION: Flat fronds form a half circle that tops a single black stem on this airy, graceful fern. In early spring the stems emerge to full height, about 12 inches tall, with the fronds crumpled against the terminal end. When the fern reaches full height, the fronds slowly spring away to form a half circle. According to Appalachian folklore, the longest frond, or finger, points to where ginseng might be found.[34]
    MPH: pp. 346-347.

HABITAT: Found in the shade in cool, damp forests. Companion plants include wild geranium (*Geranium maculatum*), trillium (*Trillium spp.*), black cohosh (*Actaea racemosa*), and blue cohosh (*Caulophyllum thalictroides*).

KEY ACTIONS: Expectorant, emmenagogue (root), febrifuge

PART USED: Fronds, root

TRADITIONAL USES: The Cherokee drank an infusion of the aerial parts of maidenhair fern to reduce fevers and to give dancers the strength to perform without tiring during long ritual dances. The root was used topically as a poultice for rheumatic pain. Dried fronds were smoked or snuffed for heart problems. The black stems were incorporated into basketry designs and used to keep pierced ears from closing up.[35] In Appalachian folk medicine, maidenhair fern was used as a soothing tea for sore throats, coughs and hoarseness.[36]

CURRENT USES: Maidenhair fern has weak medicinal properties, and the dried herb is not sold commercially. The European species, *A. capillus-veneris*, has similar properties and is available from some herb suppliers.

   Infusions soothe sore throats and hoarseness, and act as a mild expectorant to relieve coughs and respiratory congestion. The root decoction is used to bring on delayed menses.[37] A hair rinse made from the infused fronds gives a shine to dark hair.

HARVESTING: Wild maidenhair fern is at risk due to over-harvesting and habitat loss. Harvest only from known sites where the plant is abundant. Maidenhair fern plants are available from native plant nurseries and are easy to grow in the right conditions. Collect fronds anytime during the growing season. The plant dries easily.

PREPARATIONS:

◗ INFUSION: Use two tablespoons dried or one tablespoon fresh herb for each cup of water. Cover and infuse for 30 minutes. Strain.

112

♦ DECOCTION: Use one tablespoon dried chopped root to one pint water. Bring water to a boil; cover and simmer for 30 minutes. Strain.

DOSAGES: For the treatment of sore throat, cough and hoarseness, combine with other herbs that support its actions, such as mullein (*Verbascum thapsus*) or evening primrose (*Oenothera biennis*).

♦ INFUSION: Drink one cup of warm or hot infusion as needed to relieve sore throats, coughs and hoarseness.

♦ DECOCTION: Drink one pint decoction each day to bring on delayed menses.

Mountain Mint

COMMON NAME: Mountain Mint

BOTANICAL NAME: *Pycnanthemum incanum*

FAMILY: *Lamiaceae* (Mint)

OTHER NAMES: Hoary mountain mint, horsemint, wild basil

RELATED SPECIES: Appalachian mountain mint (*P. flexuosum*), Virginia mountain mint (*P. virginianum*)

DESCRIPTION: Mountain mint is a perennial, two to five feet tall, with square stems and oval, opposite leaves, with bluntly serrated edges. The fragrant leaves of young plants are tinged with red. At midsummer, the upper leaves, which are covered with fine, white hair, appear to be dusted with white powder. Lower leaves are white on the undersides only. Pale purple flowers grow in whorls at the leaf nodes in midsummer. The entire plant is delightfully aromatic.
MPH: pp. 79-80.

HABITAT: Sunny open areas and along waterways or ditches.

KEY ACTIONS: Carminative, diaphoretic, anti-spasmodic

PART USED: Aerial (in flower)

Mountain Mint - Pycnanthemum incanum

TRADITIONAL USES: The Cherokee used infusions of mountain mint to treat colds, fevers, stomach upsets, and as a penis wash to relieve inflammation. A poultice of fresh leaves was applied to the head to relieve headaches.[38]

Mountain mint has a long history of use as a folk remedy. The infusion was used to relieve indigestion, fevers, and as an inhalation for chest colds. There is also some evidence that it was a common home remedy used to bring on delayed menses.[39]

CURRENT USES: Mountain mint is a good remedy for indigestion, nausea, stomach cramps, and headaches caused by eating rich food. Hot infusions reduce fevers, and inhalations help to relieve sinus and lung congestion.

The properties of mountain mint are similar to those of more well-known members of the mint family such as peppermint (*Mentha piperata*), spearmint (*Mentha spicata*), or bee balm (*Monarda spp.*), though it has a stronger flavor.

HARVESTING: Collect mountain mint in early to mid summer. Plants should be picked in the cool of the morning, because the heat of the day dissipates the essential oils. Cut the stem just above any bug-eaten leaves. Tie together in bundles of four or five plants; hang to dry inside a paper bag in a cool place with good air circulation, or strip the leaves from the stalks and dry on a screen.

PREPARATIONS: The best way to enjoy the fragrant volatile oils of mountain mint is to prepare it as a cold infusion and reheat before drinking. By using cold water instead of hot, the floral subtleties are preserved. Hot infusions of most mints result in a harsh, acrid tea.

◖ INFUSION: Use one tablespoon of dried or two tablespoons of fresh herb for each cup of cool or room temperature water.

Cover and steep for two or more hours. Strain. Reheat as needed.

DOSAGES:

 INFUSION: Drink one cup heated infusion every few hours or as needed until symptoms improve. For a cooling summer beverage, chill mountain mint infusion in the refrigerator.

Partridgeberry

COMMON NAME: Partridgeberry

BOTANICAL NAME: *Mitchella repens*

FAMILY: *Rubiaceae* (Madder)

OTHER NAMES: Squawvine, checkerberry

DESCRIPTION: Partridgeberry is a small, perennial evergreen vine with rounded, opposite leaves that have a shiny leathery appearance. Each leaf is divided neatly in half by a white line. The entire plant is fewer than three inches high and grows in a creeping mass along the ground. Pairs of tiny white flowers have four parts and a subtle fragrance. Blooms appear in June and July. In late summer, a flavorless, mealy red berry forms and is usually eaten by birds.
    MPH: pp. 31-32.

HABITAT: Partridgeberry grows along the ground in deep woodland shade, often around the base of mountain laurel and rhododendron trees or on gradual slopes in diverse forest settings. This diminutive herb is easy to miss, as it is usually almost hidden beneath a thick layer of leaf mulch.

KEY ACTIONS: Uterine tonic, astringent

PART USED: Aerial

TRADITIONAL USES: Among American Indians, partridge berry was used as a remedy for a wide range of female reproductive system problems including menstrual cramps, delayed or irregular menses, heavy menstrual flow, labor difficulties, and infertility. Leaf infusions and poultices were used to soothe sore nipples, hemorrhoids, and wounds.[40]

The folk uses of partridgeberry include an herbal steam to relieve rheumatic pain and a decoction of the berries in milk to stop diarrhea and treat dysentery. Partridgeberry was a popular remedy for women's reproductive problems during much of the 19th and 20th centuries.[41] Though they have little flavor, the berries were also used as a food.

CURRENT USES: Partridgeberry is an important gynecological remedy in modern herbal practice. It is considered a reliable tonic to treat deficiency and weakness with symptoms such as infertility, lack of menses, menstrual pain, and threatened miscarriage. It is also an effective remedy for reducing excessively heavy menstrual flow and relieving persistent vaginal discharge. During the final trimester of pregnancy, partridgeberry is used as a uterine or labor tonic.

HARVESTING: Plants may be harvested any time of the year. Cut individual vines close to the ground, being careful not to dislodge the roots. Because partridgeberry is a very small plant, many are needed to make a significant amount of medicine. Process fresh herb or dry completely and store in a glass jar.

PREPARATIONS:

◊ TINCTURE: Fresh plant – 1:2. Dried plant: 1:5. Menstruum – 75% alcohol.

◊ DECOCTION: Use one teaspoon dried or two teaspoons fresh herb for each cup of water. Bring water to a boil; cover and simmer for 20 minutes. Strain.

DOSAGES: Partridgeberry is a tonic herb that requires three to six months of daily use for best results.

◊ TINCTURE: Take 20 to 30 drops three times a day.

◊ DECOCTION: Drink one cup three times a day.

Passionflower

COMMON NAME: Passionflower

BOTANICAL NAME: *Passiflora incarnata*

FAMILY: *Passifloraceae* (Passionflower)

OTHER NAMES: Maypop

RELATED SPECIES: Yellow passionflower (*P. lutea*)

DESCRIPTION: Passionflower is an attractive perennial vine that grows up to 20 feet long and has three- or five-lobed alternate leaves. Dramatically ornate purple flowers appear in mid summer, followed by plump oval fruits about the size of a hen's egg that turn from green to yellow when ripe. Inside the fruit, known as a maypop, are many seeds surrounded by an ambrosial, edible gel-like pulp.

Yellow passionflower (*P. lutea*) is a tiny vine with three-lobed leaves, small yellow flowers less than one-half inch in diameter, and blue-black berries. The flowers lack the botanical complexity of *P. incarnata*.

MPH: pp. 26-27, 191-192.

HABITAT: Transitional zones at the edge of forests and sunny open areas. Passionflower is a common weed throughout most of the southeast.

Passionflower - Passiflora incarnata

KEY ACTIONS: Relaxing nervine, sedative, anti-spasmodic

PART USED: Leaf, flower, fruit (edible)

TRADITIONAL USES: Cherokees collected passionflower roots and either pounded them to make a poultice or infused them for tea. The poultice was used to draw the inflammation from boils or skin infections caused by briar scratches. The infusion was used to soothe weaning babies. Drops of warm infusion were used to treat earaches. Passionflower fruits, or maypops, were crushed, and the juice was thickened with cornmeal or flour to make a pleasant beverage drink. Shoots and young leaves were cooked and eaten as a wild green.[42]

Jesuit priests who arrived in South America in the early 17th century gave passionflower its European name. They interpreted the ornate flowers as a symbol of the crucifixion and passion of Jesus Christ and as a sign that they would be successful in their mission to make converts to Christianity.

CURRENT USES: In modern herbal practice, passionflower leaf and flower are important nervine relaxants with a wide range of uses. A reliable acute remedy that counters the stressful effects of modern life, passionflower helps to relieve tension headaches and relax tight muscles. It is also used to treat insomnia, anxiety, and restlessness. Useful when excessive tension results in chest constriction, breathing difficulties, or heart palpitations. Passionflower may be effective in relieving vascular constriction that contributes to high blood pressure.

The pulp collected from inside ripe fruit is made into jelly or syrup.

HARVESTING: Collect leaves and flowers when in bloom during June and July. Gather maypop fruits after they turn pale green or

121

yellow in September and October. Yellow passionflower is rare and should not be harvested or disturbed.

PREPARATIONS:

♦ TINCTURE: Fresh – 1:2. Dried – 1:5. Menstruum – 40% alcohol.

♦ INFUSION: Use one teaspoon dried or two teaspoons fresh leaf and flower for each cup of water. Cover and infuse for 20 minutes. Strain.

DOSAGES: For best results, use small frequent doses of passionflower until symptoms improve.

♦ TINCTURE: Take 20 to 50 drops every 30 minutes until symptoms improve, or as needed.

♦ INFUSION: Drink one cup of infusion every 30 minutes until symptoms improve or as needed.

Pipsissewa

COMMON NAME: Pipsissewa

BOTANICAL NAME: *Chimaphila maculata*

FAMILY: *Ericaceae* (Heath)

OTHER NAMES: Spotted pipsissewa, rat's bane, rat's vein

RELATED SPECIES: *C. umbellata* is also known by the common name pipsissewa.

DESCRIPTION: Pipsissewa is an evergreen perennial that is only three to four inches tall. Shiny dark green leaves are leathery with sharply toothed edges. They grow in pairs or whorls and have a distinctive milky white mark along the midrib. Nodding, waxy white flowers with a pink tinge and a subtle fragrance bloom on upright stems in early summer.

The leaves of *C. umbellata* have no white markings and grow in more pronounced whorls. The flowers are also whitish pink but with red anthers.

MPH: pp. 49-51.

HABITAT: Common in dry deciduous forests.

KEY ACTIONS: Alterative, lymphatic, diuretic, tonic, antiseptic, vulnerary, anti-inflammatory

PART USED: Leaf

TRADITIONAL USES: Pipsissewa is an all-purpose remedy used to treat a wide range of health problems. The Cherokee used an infusion as a remedy for rheumatism, colds, fevers, and kidney problems. They used poultices and washes to treat ringworm, ulcers, cancer, and pain.[43]

During the Civil War era, doctors recommended pipsissewa to treat digestive problems, weak kidneys, and general debility. It was said to stimulate the appetite and revive flagging energy. Infusions were used internally and externally to heal obstinate ulcers. Leaves were soaked in whiskey to make a rheumatism remedy that warmed the joints and relieved stiffness and pain.

Folk usage of pipsissewa includes combining it with mullein leaf (*Verbascum thapsus*) to keep children from wetting the bed, and as a spring tonic and a general energy booster. Pipsissewa root was an ingredient in traditional root beer. According to Southern folklore, pipsissewa will repel or kill rats, hence the common name "rat's bane."

CURRENT USES: In modern herbal practice, pipsissewa is a standard remedy to treat acute and chronic urinary tract problems. It is an effective tonic for chronic kidney problems that include a pattern of frequent bladder infections, incontinence, or a history of kidney disease. Pipsissewa is also used to treat acute kidney problems such as: bladder infections, prostatitis, cystitis and urethritis, blood or pus in the urine, kidney stones, and painful or frequent urination. The infusion is used as a douche to relieve vaginal discharges.

HARVESTING: Gather pipsissewa leaves any time of year. Cut the stem just above the ground; strip leaves from the stem, and rinse well. Dry or process fresh. Because pipsissewa is so small, many plants are needed.

Although the leaves are recognized as the most medicinally potent part of the plant, the entire plant, including the roots, is used in Southern folk medicine.

PREPARATIONS:

◊ TINCTURE: Fresh – 1:2. Dried – 1:5. Menstruum – 50% alcohol.

◊ INFUSION: Use one tablespoon dried or two tablespoons fresh leaf for each cup of water. Cover and steep for 30 minutes. Strain.

DOSAGES: Any acute kidney symptoms (listed above) may indicate a kidney infection, especially when accompanied by sharp pain and fever. A kidney infection is life-threatening. If these symptoms occur, immediately seek an accurate diagnosis from a medical professional trained to diagnose acute kidney infections before attempting to treat with herbs.

◊ TINCTURE: For acute symptoms, take 20 drops every hour. As a tonic, take 20 to 40 drops three times a day for a month or longer.

◊ INFUSION: For acute symptoms, drink one-half cup every hour. As a tonic, drink three cups a day for one month or longer.

Pleurisy Root

COMMON NAME: Pleurisy Root

BOTANICAL NAME: *Asclepias tuberosa*

FAMILY: *Asclepiadaceae* (Milkweed)

OTHER NAMES: Butterfly weed, colic root

DESCRIPTION: Pleurisy root is a perennial, two to three feet tall, with narrow, short leaves arranged alternately along a thick, slightly hairy stem. Distinctive fluorescent orange flowers bloom in irregular clusters from June to August. Individual flowers have five sepals, five petals (that curve sharply downward), and five coronas. The flowers are very fragrant, and their nectar is sweet. Seed pods are shaped like a big green teardrop, two to four inches long, and have a bumpy surface. When ripe, the pod cracks open, and brown seeds, each attached to their own silky, down-like navigational system, are dispersed by the wind. Pleurisy root is part of a large plant family of over 2,000 species, mostly found in tropical climates.
MPH: p. 154.

HABITAT: Look for pleurisy root in sunny, open areas and in transitional zones at the edge of forests and along roads.

KEY ACTIONS: Stimulating expectorant, bronchial dilator, anti-inflammatory, anti-spasmodic, anti-catarrhal, lymphatic, cardio-stimulant

PART USED: Root

TRADITIONAL USES: Pleurisy root has been an important remedy in American Indian and folk medicine for the treatment of respiratory and pulmonary problems. It was considered a specific remedy for chest complaints, coughing, congestion, and breathing difficulties and was used in combination with other herbs in the treatment of bronchitis, pleurisy, and pneumonia. Pleurisy root was also used for pulmonary edema to move fluids out of the chest in order to improve heart function.

The leaves are an important food source for monarch butterflies. While in the caterpillar stage, monarch butterflies feed on the leaves of pleurisy root. The leaves contain toxic alkaloids that the caterpillars store in their bodies. Later, after caterpillars metamorphose into butterflies, these alkaloids make ingesting the butterflies toxic to birds. To ward off predatory birds, several other butterfly species mimic the monarch's appearance, although they do not feed on pleurisy root and do not harbor the poisonous chemicals. The flowers are also an important food source for adult monarchs and swallowtails, among others.

CURRENT USES: Pleurisy root is still used in the treatment of the respiratory system; however, attention to proper dosage is essential. As a bronchial dilator and stimulating expectorant, pleurisy root relieves breathing difficulties and effectively breaks up and eliminates lung congestion. It is a specific treatment for colds, chest infections, bronchitis, pleurisy, and pneumonia. Pleurisy root also improves lymphatic drainage and resolves mild pulmonary edema.

HARVESTING: Harvest the root in the fall after the seed is ripe. Pleurisy root has a thick taproot that is notoriously hard to extract from the ground; it seems to wedge itself into the hardest earth available. Immediately after harvesting, clean and slice the root into small pieces. Dry completely.

PREPARATIONS: Use dried roots only.

♦ TINCTURE: Dried root –1:5. Menstruum – 50% alcohol.

♦ DECOCTION: Use one teaspoon dried root for each cup of water. Bring water to a boil; cover and simmer for 10 minutes. Strain.

DOSAGES: Pleurisy root should only be used for short periods of time to treat acute symptoms. Large doses may cause vomiting and nausea. Reduce the dosage or discontinue use if stomach upset occurs. Not to be used during pregnancy.

♦ TINCTURE: Take 20 drops in a small amount of water three times a day.

♦ DECOCTION: Drink one cup hot decoction three times a day.

Rabbit Tobacco

COMMON NAME: Rabbit Tobacco

BOTANICAL NAME: *Gnaphalium obtusifolium*

FAMILY: *Asteraceae* (Aster)

OTHER NAMES: Sweet everlasting, life everlasting

DESCRIPTION: Rabbit tobacco is a biennial herb, one to three feet tall, with gray-green foliage. From July to October, dingy white flowers bloom in ragged clusters at the top of the plant. Leaves are alternate, lance-shaped and without stalks. The entire plant has a pleasant pungent aroma.
  MPH: p. 94.

HABITAT: Open, sunny areas.

KEY ACTIONS: Sedative, analgesic, expectorant, anti-spasmodic, astringent

PART USED: Aerial (in flower)

TRADITIONAL USES: Rabbit tobacco has a long history as a remedy for both physical and psychological imbalances. American Indians relied on rabbit tobacco for general pain relief and as a muscle relaxant. It was used extensively for respiratory problems

129

including coughs and colds, lung pain, and sore throats. The dried herb was smoked to relieve asthmatic symptoms and as a sedative. Rabbit tobacco was also burned as a smudge or used as a wash to treat persons bothered by ghosts or those who "wanted to run away."[44]

CURRENT USES: Rabbit tobacco has a mixed reputation as an effective medicine. Although it is a staple home remedy in many areas, it seems to have only mild therapeutic properties. Herbalist Tommie Bass used it in inhalations for colds, sinus infections, asthma and coughs. He put the plants in the kitchen sink, ran hot water over them, and had people inhale the vapors.[45]

Infusions are used as a sedative and to relieve chest pain, congestion, and inflammation. Rabbit tobacco is a traditional ingredient in cough syrup formulas along with other expectorants such as wild cherry bark (*Prunus serotina*), sweet gum resin (*Liquidambar styraciflua*), maidenhair fern (*Adiantum pedatum*), and mullein (*Verbascum thapsus*).

Dried rabbit tobacco is used in inhalations or smoked to relieve coughs, asthma symptoms, lung congestion and pain, and nervousness.

HARVESTING: Collect the entire plant when in bloom. Bundle stems and hang to dry. When leaves crumble to the touch, strip leaves and flowers from the stem and store in a jar.

PREPARATIONS:

⧫ INHALATION: Using a wide ceramic bowl, prepare a simple infusion by steeping a generous handful of dried rabbit tobacco in two pints of freshly boiled water. Make a tent by draping a tablecloth or bath towel over your head and the bowl; inhale the vapors from the steaming infusion for 10 minutes.

- INFUSION: Use one tablespoon dried rabbit tobacco for each cup of water. Cover and steep for 20 minutes. Strain and sweeten.

- HERBAL SMOKE INHALATION: Grind or crush dried leaf and flower as finely as possible. Fill a pipe with herb and ignite.

DOSAGES:

- INHALATION: Use an inhalation every two to three hours to relieve acute respiratory congestion or until symptoms improve.

- INFUSION: Drink three to four cups of tea each day until symptoms improve.

- HERBAL SMOKE INHALATION: Inhale deeply and hold the smoke for several seconds before exhaling. Repeat two or three times or as needed to relieve symptoms. Don't overuse smoking therapies, because they can dry the lungs.

Red Root

COMMON NAME: Red Root

BOTANICAL NAME: *Ceanothus americanus*

FAMILY: *Rhamnaceae* (Buckthorn)

OTHER NAMES: New Jersey tea, redshank

DESCRIPTION: Red root is a small shrub, two to four feet tall, with oval, serrated opposite leaves. Three prominent veins begin at the base of each leaf and continue along to the outer margin and tip. Clusters of tiny white flowers with five petals bloom from May to September.
    MPH: pp. 277-278.

HABITAT: Common throughout the region in sunny open areas and in transition zones along the edges of forests. Usually thrives in dry, rocky soil. Companion plants include elder (*Sambucus canadensis*), mullein (*Verbascum thapsus*) and various brambles.

KEY ACTIONS: Lymphatic, alterative, astringent, nervine

PART USED: Root, leaf

TRADITIONAL USES: Root decoction was used to relieve constipation with symptoms of bloating and shortness of breath. The

Cherokee used the tea as a mouthwash to relieve toothaches. Leaves were used as a beverage tea.[46]

Appalachian folk medicine used red root as a gargle for sore throats, thrush and oral inflammation. Tommie Bass used a decoction of the root to treat prostate inflammation, psoriasis, and glandular swellings.[47]

CURRENT USES: Red root is an important remedy used to treat liver and lymphatic congestion. It is a specific treatment for symptoms of congestion and inflammation of the pelvis such as leucorrhea, menstrual cramping, and prostatitis. Use red root to stimulate the lymphatic system and relieve swollen lymph glands or fibrocystic breast disease. Use leaf infusion or root decoction as an astringent wash for eruptive, weeping skin conditions and as a first aid treatment for burns.

HARVESTING: Harvest the root in spring or after the flowers have faded. Cut the root into small pieces immediately after harvesting, because it is impossible to cut after it dries. Leaves may be collected anytime during the growing season and dried for use as a beverage tea.

PREPARATIONS:

◆ TINCTURE: Fresh root – 1:2. Dried root – 1:5. Menstruum – 60% alcohol.

◆ DECOCTION: Use one teaspoon dried or two teaspoons fresh root for each cup of water. Bring to a boil; cover and simmer for 20 minutes. Strain.

◆ INFUSION: Use one teaspoon dried leaves per cup of water. Cover and infuse for five minutes or to taste.

DOSAGES: Red root is usually used in small, regular doses taken over several weeks or months to address long-standing problems such as fibrocystic breast disease or prostatitis.

◆ TINCTURE: Take 20 to 30 drops three times a day for several weeks or months. To relieve acute symptoms, take up to 50 drops three times a day.

◆ DECOCTION: Drink one to two cups of root decoction per day for several weeks or months. Use externally as a skin wash.

◆ INFUSION: Drink leaf infusion as a beverage tea. Use externally as a skin wash.

Sarsaparilla

COMMON NAME: Sarsaparilla

BOTANICAL NAME: *Aralia nudicaulis*

FAMILY: *Araliaceae* (Ginseng)

OTHER NAMES: American sarsaparilla, wild sarsaparilla, spikenard

RELATED SPECIES: Two other plants found throughout the region, *Smilax glauca* and *S. rotundifolia*, are also known by the common name "sarsaparilla." They are also called catbrier, sawbrier, and greenbrier. Their medicinal properties differ from *A. nudicaulis.*

DESCRIPTION: Sarsaparilla is a perennial, about two feet tall, with compound leaves arranged in groups of three to five per stem. Individual leaves are oval with toothed margins. Small white flowers bloom just below the leaves, from June to August. In the fall, clusters of wine-colored, slightly translucent berries appear. When ripe, they have a spicy, tart flavor. Thick, fleshy roots grow horizontally just below the surface of the ground.
   MPH: p. 63.

HABITAT: Common in dense woods along creeks, swamps and other wetland areas. Frequently found growing on shaded hillsides

135

surrounded by black cohosh (*Actaea racemosa*) and blue cohosh (*Caulophyllum thalictroides*). Sarsaparilla plants grow in widely spaced stands of two or three plants.

KEY ACTIONS: Stimulant, alterative, tonic

PART USED: Root, berries (edible)

TRADITIONAL USES: In North America, the Cherokee and other American Indians considered sarsaparilla a panacea and used it alone or combined it with other herbs to treat symptoms of weakness. Sarsaparilla root decoction was given to children to treat pneumonia, teething sickness, and kidney weakness. It was used externally to treat infections of the skin and mouth.[48]

During the 16th century, sarsaparilla was one of the many New World remedies that caused a sensation in Europe, where it was used to treat pulmonary problems and syphilis. In North America, sarsaparilla was used as a blood purifier to treat a wide range of chronic diseases.

This pleasant tasting herb was one of the main ingredients in original root beer recipes.

CURRENT USES: Sarsaparilla is not widely used in modern herbal practice. It is considered weaker than American ginseng (*Panax quinquefolius*), although it addresses some of the same health issues. Sarsaparilla is used as a mild tonic for fatigue. It acts as a restorative for the entire body and is recommended following long periods of stress, overwork, or serious illness. Sarsaparilla, combined with other lung herbs, is used to treat respiratory infections. It moistens and strengthens the lungs and is a specific remedy for lingering dry coughs following bronchitis or respiratory infections. Sarsaparilla is a pleasant tasting tea that may be used daily as a general tonic.

HARVESTING: Harvest roots in the fall after the berries have ripened. Thick, fleshy sarsaparilla roots grow horizontally just below the ground. Before digging the root, clear away dirt and leaves from around the base of the main stem; then dig carefully into the dirt, using your hands as needed, to determine which direction the root is growing. Unearth by digging dirt away from either side of the root, following the shape of the root, and then lifting it out of the ground. Wash and slice the fresh root immediately after harvest.

PREPARATIONS: Tincture made with freshly harvested root is best.

⬧ TINCTURE: Fresh root – 1:2. Dried root – 1:5. Menstruum – 50% alcohol.

⬧ DECOCTION: Use one tablespoon dried root or two tablespoons fresh root for each cup of water. Bring to a boil; cover and simmer for 20 minutes. Strain.

DOSAGES:

⬧ TINCTURE: As a general tonic, take 30 to 50 drops in a small amount of water, two to three times a day for one month or longer.

⬧ DECOCTION: As a general tonic, drink two to three cups of decoction per day for one month or longer.

Sassafras

COMMON NAME: Sassafras

BOTANICAL NAME: *Sassafras albidum*

FAMILY: *Lauraceae* (Laurel)

OTHER NAMES: Cinnamon wood, ague tree

DESCRIPTION: Sassafras trees can reach up to 40 or more feet in height and are common in deciduous forests. The bark is furrowed and creased with horizontal ridges and cracks. Leaves are lobed and grow in three distinctive shapes: footballs or ovals, mittens, and ghosts or tridents. Tiny clusters of sessile yellow flowers bloom along the branches in April and May. Small, blue, egg-shaped fruits, containing one seed each, form in late summer. Dense, woody roots grow horizontally just under the ground away from the trunk. All parts of the sassafras are aromatic and when crushed or bruised release a pleasant cinnamon-like fragrance.
MPH: p. 314.

HABITAT: Common throughout deciduous forests of eastern North America. Grows well in any kind of soil. Mature trees are often surrounded by saplings of various sizes that rarely reach maturity in the dense forest shade.

KEY ACTIONS: Carminative, demulcent, alterative, diaphoretic

PART USED: Root bark, bark, leaf (pith)

TRADITIONAL USES: American Indians used sassafras as a beverage, cooking spice, and medicine. It was considered a blood tonic and was used for a wide range of conditions believed to be caused by toxins or heat in the blood, such as rheumatism, hives, measles, skin eruptions, and rashes. Infusions of the bark were also used to treat diarrhea, worms, and parasites.[49]

Sassafras was a popular beverage tea. The dried leaves were powdered and used as spice for meats and as a thickening agent for soups and stews. The Choctaws of Louisiana are credited with teaching French settlers how to use the dried, powdered leaves to thicken a stew now known as "file gumbo," a classic Creole dish.

Sassafras has a long history of use as a folk remedy in the southern Appalachians where it is still used as a traditional spring tonic to thin the blood after many months without fresh fruits and vegetables. The pith, or spongy, inner layer of the outermost branches, is dissolved in water to make a soothing wash for sore eyes. Hot sassafras root tea is drunk to relieve fevers from colds and influenza.

Until recently, sassafras was used as a flavoring agent in commercial root beer.

CURRENT USES: Sassafras is rarely used in modern herbal practice. In the United States, it is banned from sale in commercial preparations. Safrole, a compound in sassafras essential oil, was classified as a carcinogen by the Food and Drug Administration based on the results of an experiment in which huge amounts of concentrated synthetic safrole were fed to rats that later developed cancer. No known human cases of toxicity have been documented, and the occasional use of sassafras tea is considered safe.

Sassafras is a gentle yet effective alterative useful in the treatment of chronic skin conditions such as eczema and psoriasis.

When used as a tonic to cool and detoxify the blood, it also helps relieve symptoms of rheumatism or gout.

The carminative qualities of sassafras make it a reliable digestive system remedy. It quickly relieves nausea, indigestion, and gas. Sipping small amounts of sassafras tea can stop vomiting and soothe symptoms of Irritable Bowel Syndrome. Sassafras is sometimes used as an ingredient in alterative or hepatic tea formulas, because it has a pleasant flavor that helps mask bitter herbs.

Sassafras decoction makes an effective diaphoretic tea to reduce fevers and relieve congestion caused by colds and flu. Root bark decoction is used as a wash to relieve poison ivy rash.

HARVESTING: Sassafras root bark is harvested January through March. It may be necessary to mark sassafras trees with colored yarn in the fall so they can be easily identified in the winter. The root bark of full-grown trees is sometimes harvested by digging the surface roots that lie just below the drip line, or outermost edges of the branches that extend farthest from the trunk. Because many roots crisscross just beneath the soil's surface in the forest, an easier way to collect sassafras root is to identify saplings that have sprouted up around mature trees. There are usually many small sassafras saplings within a 30-foot radius of an established tree. Their roots are small and easy to dig up.

Sassafras roots grow horizontally from the base of the trunk. Before digging, determine which direction the root extends away from the trunk. Once the soil is loosened around the base of the sapling, the root can usually be pulled up. Cut away the root from the trunk and wash immediately. If the root is bigger than one inch in diameter, use a knife to scrape the bark off the root. For smaller roots, simply cut into pieces. Dry the bark scrapings or sliced root. Roots turn rich reddish brown when dry.

Collect bark from the trunk of saplings in early spring just as leaves begin to appear. Do not collect bark from mature trees, because it makes them vulnerable to disease and often kills them. Gather green leaves in June through August. Once the leaves begin to turn yellow in early autumn, they lose their potency.

PREPARATIONS: In order to avoid any real or imagined dangers associated with safrole, only use sassafras infusions or decoctions. Avoid essential oils or tinctures. Consider adding sassafras leaf or root to tea formulas to improve flavor and mask the taste of unpleasant herbs.

♦ DECOCTION: Use one teaspoon dried or two teaspoons fresh root for every cup of water. Bring to a boil; cover and simmer for 10 minutes. Strain. Sweeten if desired.

♦ INFUSION: Use one tablespoon dried leaves or six to eight fresh crushed leaves for each cup of water. Cover and steep for 30 minutes. Strain.

DOSAGES: Do not drink sassafras tea daily for more than three weeks. Sassafras should not be used during pregnancy or with children under seven years of age.

♦ DECOCTION/INFUSION: Drink one to two cups of leaf infusion or root decoction each day for a week or as needed.

Skullcap

COMMON NAME: Skullcap

BOTANICAL NAME: *Scutellaria lateriflora*

FAMILY: *Lamiaceae* (Mint)

OTHER NAMES: Mad dog skullcap

DESCRIPTION: Skullcap is an upright perennial herb, one to two feet tall, with a square stem and opposite leaves that are slightly toothed and lance-shaped. Pale blue flowers bloom between June and September on racemes that emerge at the leaf axis. Flowers only grow on one side of the raceme or flower stalk. Although skullcap is a member of the mint family, it is bitter tasting and lacks the characteristic mint flavor.
MPH: pp. 210-211.

HABITAT: Common along the edges of sunny open areas where the ground is slightly damp.

KEY ACTIONS: Nervine, anti-spasmodic, nerve tonic, bitter

PART USED: Aerial (in flower)

TRADITIONAL USES: The Cherokee used skullcap to treat women's reproductive system problems such as menstrual cramping, delayed menses, and breast tenderness or pain. A strong tea preparation was given to women immediately after labor to induce vomiting, with the belief that this would help expel the afterbirth.[50]

Throughout the region, skullcap was used as a folk remedy for mad dog bites and hydrophobia. It was also regarded as a potent restorative to treat symptoms of nervous exhaustion accompanied by insomnia, depression, anxiety, and muscle tremors or spasms.

CURRENT USES: Skullcap is a versatile nervine that is useful to treat a wide range of nervous system imbalances. Skullcap is a specific remedy for mental fatigue and nervous exhaustion caused by over-stimulation and the effects of long-term stress. It is also used to treat insomnia, migraine headaches and anxiety. As an antispasmodic, it relieves menstrual cramping, general muscle tension, sciatic and back pain. Skullcap has also been used to ease the symptoms of drug and alcohol withdrawal.

HARVESTING: Collect skullcap plants when in full bloom in mid to late summer. Cut the stem just above any dried or bug-eaten leaves. To dry, bundle five or six plants together with a rubber band and hang to dry. When leaves crumble to the touch, strip the leaves and flowers from the stems, chop the dried stems, and store in a glass jar.

PREPARATIONS: Skullcap is used either as a tincture or infusion.

◗ TINCTURE: Fresh herb – 1:2. Menstruum – 75% alcohol. Dried herb – 1:5. Menstruum – 50% alcohol.

◗ INFUSION: Use one teaspoon dried or two teaspoons fresh herb for each cup of water. Cover and steep for 15 minutes. Strain.

DOSAGES: Skullcap works as both an activator to relieve acute symptoms and as a tonic to restore the nervous system. Vary the dosage to achieve the desired effect.

- TINCTURE: For acute conditions, take 20 to 40 drops every 30 to 60 minutes or as needed. To use as a tonic, take 20 drops two to three times a day for a month or longer.

- INFUSION: For acute conditions, drink one cup every 30 minutes or as needed. To use skullcap as a nerve tonic, drink two to four cups each day for a month or longer.

Solomon's Seal

COMMON NAME: Solomon's Seal

BOTANICAL NAME: *Polygonatum biflorum*

FAMILY: *Liliaceae* (Lily)

OTHER NAMES: True Solomon's seal, High John the Conqueror, King Solomon's seal

RELATED SPECIES: Hairy Solomon's seal (*P. pubescens*), Solomon's plume or false Solomon's seal (*Smilacina racemosa*)

DESCRIPTION: Solomon's seal is a perennial, one to two feet tall, with oval, alternate leaves and parallel veins evenly spaced along a graceful arching stem. Slightly hidden tubular whitish-yellow flowers dangle from each leaf axil along the length of the stem. Solomon's seal blooms May to June. As they ripen in late summer, berries change from green to dark blue.

Solomon's seal takes its name from the round stem scars on the rootstock that resemble a wax seal marked with an "S." The rhizome grows horizontally just beneath the ground. It is knobby and rounded with delicate root hairs along its length. Stem scars or "seals" indicate the age of the plant, one scar for each year of growth. The white bud found at the terminal end of each rhizome, along with a bit of the root, may be replanted to generate a new plant.

Hairy Solomon's seal (*P. pubescens*) is slightly smaller than *P. biflorum*. The underside of the leaf has fine hair along each vein.

Solomon's plume or false Solomon's seal (*Smilacina racemosa*) is often found growing near Solomon's seal, and the two plants are sometimes confused. Solomon's plume has a distinctive zigzag stem, small star-like flowers that bloom in a terminal cluster from May to July, and red berries.

MPH: pp. 36-37.

HABITAT: Deciduous forests throughout the region. Solomon's seal favors cool moist slopes. Often found near maidenhair fern (*Adiantum pedatum*), black cohosh (*Actaea racemosa*), blue cohosh (*Caulophyllum thalictroides*), bloodroot (*Sanguinaria canadensis*), and trillium (*Trillium spp.*)

KEY ACTIONS: Demulcent, expectorant, sedative, tonic

PART USED: Root

TRADITIONAL USES: American Indians used Solomon's seal as both food and medicine. Edible young shoots were collected in spring and added to soups and stews. Roasted roots were ground to make flour. Crushed, fresh roots were applied as a poultice to bruises and swellings. Strong decoctions of the root were taken for lung problems such as consumption, coughs, breathing difficulties and chronic lung weakness. This same preparation was used to treat inflammation of the stomach and bowels.

Solomon's seal also has a long history as an herb with magical properties. American Indians burned the root to clean sleeping quarters and guarantee restful sleep.[51] Among African Americans, the dried root was known as "High John the Conqueror root" and considered a powerful talisman that brings good fortune and protection from evil. This belief is still held today in some areas of the South.

CURRENT USES: Solomon's seal is used in Traditional Chinese Medicine, where it is known as *Yu Zhu*.

Tea from the decocted roots soothes inflammation and irritation of the lungs, stomach, and intestinal tract. Use Solomon's seal as a mild tonic for general debility and weakness, especially after a long illness when symptoms such as lack of appetite, a dry hacking cough and restlessness are present. Fresh root poultice is applied to bruises.

HARVESTING: Dig roots in the late summer or early fall after berries ripen. Discard leaf and berries. Wash roots, cut into pieces and dry on a screen in a warm place.

PREPARATIONS: Use fresh root to make a poultice. Dry the root for use in decoctions.

- DECOCTION: Use two tablespoons dried root for each pint of water. Bring to a boil; cover and simmer for 20 minutes. Strain.

- POULTICE: Take freshly harvested roots and chop into small pieces. Use a mortar and pestle to pound into a paste. Add a little aloe vera gel if needed to make a smooth mixture that holds together. Use immediately.

DOSAGES:

- DECOCTION: Drink one cup three or four times a day.

- POULTICE: Apply as needed to relieve pain and swelling from bruises.

Spicebush

COMMON NAME: Spicebush

BOTANICAL NAME: *Lindera benzoin*

FAMILY: *Lauraceae* (Laurel)

OTHER NAMES: Wild allspice, spicewood

DESCRIPTION: Spicebush is a deciduous shrub, five to seven feet tall, with alternate, oval leaves. Small clusters of yellow flowers bloom in early spring before the leaves emerge. In the fall, spicebush has shiny hard red berries, each containing only one seed. The berries have a spicy taste, and all parts of the plant are aromatic.
 MPH: pp. 282-283.

HABITAT: Understory plant in deciduous forests. Often found growing along streams and creeks.

KEY ACTIONS: Diaphoretic, stimulant, aromatic, expectorant

PART USED: Leaf, bark, twig, berry

TRADITIONAL USES: American Indians made tea from all parts of the spicebush. They drank the tea as a spring tonic, and to treat coughs, fevers, and measles. Spicebush was also used to bring on delayed menses.[52] During the Civil War, spicebush was considered a substitute for allspice, and the berries were used as an aromatic seasoning.

CURRENT USES: Spicebush is rarely used in modern herbal practice. However, a hot decoction made from twigs, leaves, and bark is an effective diaphoretic for the treatment of respiratory infections, colds and fever. The tea can also be used to relieve menstrual cramps, bring on delayed menses, and as a general tonic. Spicebush leaves and twigs are a pleasant tasting beverage tea.

HARVESTING: Harvest leaves, bark, and twigs anytime, though they are most potent during early spring to mid summer. Collect small twigs from the outer branches, or strip the bark from thicker branches, and dry. Harvest berries as soon as they turn deep scarlet in early fall. Prepare according to directions below.

PREPARATIONS:

- DECOCTION: Use one-half cup dried or one-fourth cup of finely chopped fresh leaves and twigs for each cup of water. Bring to a boil; cover and simmer for at least 20 minutes. Strain and sweeten.

- CONDIMENT: Berries are difficult to dry. Foraging expert Steve Brill recommends chopping the berries (including the seed) in a food processor and then flash-freezing them on a cookie sheet. Store frozen berries in a bag or jar in the freezer. Use fresh or frozen berries to flavor apple, pumpkin or squash pies, applesauce, apple cider, or any recipe that calls for allspice or cinnamon.

DOSAGES:

◊ DECOCTION: Drink one cup of hot decoction two to four times a day.

Stoneroot

COMMON NAME: Stoneroot

BOTANICAL NAME: *Collinsonia canadensis*

FAMILY: *Lamiaceae* (Mint)

OTHER NAMES: Rich weed, horsemint, horseweed, horsebalm

DESCRIPTION: Stoneroot is a perennial plant, two to four feet high, with a square stem and opposite leaves. The leaf is large with serrated edges. Lower leaves have a short stem, or petiole, while the leaves at the top of the plant are attached directly to the stem (sessile). Flowers grow in upright racemes at the top of the plant, and bloom July to August. The flowers are a pale greenish-yellow with two lips (the lower lip is fringed) and have a slightly pungent lemon fragrance. The entire plant is aromatic.
MPH: pp. 126-127.

HABITAT: Grows in deep shade in damp cool areas. Often found along streambeds along with yellowroot (*Xanthorhiza simplicissima*) and wild geranium (*Geranium maculatum*).

KEY ACTIONS: Anti-lithic, diaphoretic, circulatory stimulant, anti-inflammatory, vascular tonic

PART USED: Entire plant (in flower)

TRADITIONAL USES: American Indians used stoneroot as a poultice or as a wash to relieve swollen breasts, headaches, and rheumatic pains. The infusion was used to relieve kidney and heart problems and to cure listlessness in children. Flowers and leaves were used as a deodorant.[53]

CURRENT USES: Stoneroot is a complex remedy used to treat a wide range of symptoms. It resolves vascular constriction in the pelvis and rectum that results in a sensation of heaviness and bearing down in the rectal area. Specific conditions include hemorrhoids, prostatitis, anal fistulas, and rectal pain. Stoneroot's anti-inflammatory properties soothe the upper respiratory system and are an effective remedy for laryngitis. When used in tonic doses, stoneroot helps prevent the formation of kidney stones and gallstones. It also acts as a gentle stimulant to the heart and is often combined with cardiovascular tonics in the treatment of heart disease.

HARVESTING: Harvest the entire plant, including the root, while in flower in mid to late summer. Immediately clean the root and cut into small pieces. Once it dries, even slightly, the significance of the common name "stoneroot" becomes evident.

PREPARATIONS: Tincture prepared from the entire fresh plant is the best way to use stoneroot.

- ◆ TINCTURE: Fresh plant – 1:2. Menstruum – 50% alcohol.

- ◆ DECOCTION: Use one to two teaspoons dried chopped herb for each cup of water. Bring to a boil; cover and simmer for 15 minutes. Strain.

DOSAGES:

- ❦ TINCTURE: Take 10 to 20 drops three to four times a day.

- ❦ DECOCTION: Drink one cup of warm decoction three times a day.

Sumac

COMMON NAME: Sumac

BOTANICAL NAME: *Rhus glabra*

FAMILY: *Anacardiaceae* (Cashew)

OTHER NAMES: Smooth sumac

RELATED SPECIES: Flameleaf or winged sumac (*R. copallina*), staghorn sumac (*R. typhina*)

DESCRIPTION: Three species of sumac with similar medicinal properties grow throughout the region. Though all are small shrubs or trees, four to 30 feet tall, which grow in thickets, each species differs slightly in appearance.

The compound leaves of smooth sumac (*R. glabra*) are composed of about 13 sharply toothed leaflets, each about two inches long, with a red rib and white undersides. The leaves and stalks are smooth and hairless. Those of flameleaf or winged sumac (*R. copallina*) are shiny with a distinctive winged midrib along the stem between each leaflet. Staghorn sumac (*R. typhina*) has the largest leaves—up to 24 inches long—with sharply toothed leaflets; the leaves and branches are covered with fine downy hair.

In midsummer all three species have clusters of tiny, upright, greenish-yellow flowers that ripen into hard, round, red berries covered with fine hair. As autumn progresses, sumac berries gradually turn from brilliant scarlet to muted rust. At the onset of cold weather, the leaves of all sumac species put on a dramatic flame-red display. The forked zigzag of bare sumac branches resembles a stag's horn silhouetted against the winter sky.

Poison sumac (*R. vernix*) has toothless compound leaves with big spaces between the leaflets and hanging clusters of white berries. It causes severe rashes.

MPH: pp. 280-282.

HABITAT: Common along roadsides and the edges of fields.

KEY ACTIONS: Astringent, styptic, refrigerant

PART USED: Leaf, berry, bark

TRADITIONAL USES: American Indians used almost every part of sumac. The leaves, bark, and berries were decocted or infused to make an astringent wash to treat burns, stop bleeding (internal and external), control diarrhea, and reduce fever. The leaves were also used for tanning leather. The berries produce a rich black dye. After sumac leaves turned red in the fall, they were collected, dried, and mixed with tobacco in ceremonial smoking blends. Ripe berries were infused in water to make a cooling lemony beverage.[54]

Alabama herbalist Tommie Bass considered the sumac berry to be an important source of vitamin C. He recommended using berry tea as a gargle for sore throats or as a compress for hemorrhoids.[55]

During the Civil War, a black shoe polish called "shoemac" was made from the leaf.[56]

CURRENT USES: Sumac is not commonly used in herbal practice, though it is a potent folk remedy. Infusions of sumac berry or leaf make an effective tea for relieving cold symptoms such as coughs and fevers. The tea is also a fast-acting remedy for diarrhea. Berry or leaf infusion is used topically to cool burns, clean wounds, stop bleeding, and as a douche to treat vaginal discharge. As a gargle, it is used to treat sore throats, mouth sores or inflamed gums.

Powdered sumac berries are available commercially for culinary use; they are a traditional spice in Middle Eastern cooking. Wild food enthusiasts have made sumac berry lemonade a popular thirst-quenching trail beverage.

HARVESTING: Harvest leaves in mid summer just as the flower begins to bloom. Gather sumac berries before the first frost when the vitamin C levels are highest, and the berries are still brilliant red.

PREPARATIONS: Infusions of sumac berries or leaves are the most common way to use this plant as a medicine. Do not decoct or infuse sumac for any longer than the times recommended here, or the mixture will be too astringent to use internally. Sumac leaves and berries can also be used to make cough syrup. (See recipe included under "Wild Cherry".)

◗ INFUSION: Use one-half cup dried or one full cup of fresh, loosely packed leaves for each quart of boiling water. Cover and steep for 10 minutes. Strain.

Use two clusters of crushed ripe berries for each quart of cool water. Crush berries by placing them in a medium-sized bowl and pressing them firmly with the back of a wooden spoon. Cover and steep for 10 minutes. Strain berry infusion through a colander lined with muslin to remove fine hairs from the berries before drinking.

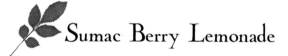Sumac Berry Lemonade

While not strictly a medicinal preparation, sumac berry lemonade is a refreshing cure for the heat of hot summer afternoons. Sumac berry infusion is also served hot to relieve cold symptoms.

Place four to five clusters of ripe, fresh sumac berries in a gallon container. Crush berries using a wooden spoon, then cover with one gallon of cool water. Swirl the berries around in the water for a few minutes. Strain the mixture through a colander lined with a piece of cotton muslin. Careful straining is needed to remove the fine hairs from the berries.

Sweeten the infusion with honey or mix with fruit juices. In warm weather, chill before serving.

DOSAGES: Because sumac is high in tannins, it should not be used internally for more than a few days by people with a history of kidney stones.

 INFUSION: Drink one cup of infusion every hour until symptoms improve. Warm infusion is also used as a gargle for throat inflammation and pain. Use cool infusion as needed as a wash to treat burns or wounds, and as a douche to relieve vaginal discharge.

Sweet Gum

COMMON NAME: Sweet Gum

BOTANICAL NAME: *Liquidambar styraciflua*

FAMILY: *Hamamelidaceae* (Witch Hazel)

DESCRIPTION: Sweet gum is a large tree, sometimes reaching over 100 feet tall, with sharply palmate, star-shaped leaves that have five to seven lobes. Round fruits, one and a half inches in diameter, are green in the spring, ripen to a dull brown in the fall, and are covered with short spikes encircling tube-like indentations. After the leaves have fallen, the ripe fruits look like ornaments dangling from the branches. Sweet gum is one of the first trees to change color in the fall. Leaves have a pine scent when crushed. Strange-looking wing-like ridges protrude from along the outermost branches. Look for resinous gum or sap oozing from the bark.
    MPH: p. 315.

HABITAT: Usually found growing along streams or in other wet areas.

KEY ACTIONS: Expectorant, antiseptic, astringent, sedative

PART USED: Resin (gum), leaf, inner bark

TRADITIONAL USES: Among American Indians, sweet gum resin was used as an ingredient in skin salves to treat itching, wounds, boils, and ulcers. The resin and inner bark were used to make an astringent tea to relieve diarrhea, fevers, and excessive menstrual bleeding. There is also some evidence that bark tea was used to relieve anxiety.[57] For generations, sweet gum resin has been a popular chewing gum.[58]

Civil War doctors decocted the inner bark in milk to make a remedy for diarrhea and dysentery.

Alabama herbalist Tommie Bass burned sweet gum fruit and added the ash to lard or tallow to make a skin salve.[59]

CURRENT USES: Sweet gum resin is a valuable remedy for respiratory congestion and chest colds, though it is rarely available on the commercial herb market. Sweet gum resin and bark are effective expectorants used in cough syrups, and small lumps of resin may be chewed to treat sore throat pain. A decoction made from the bark and leaf settles the stomach and relieves lung congestion. Bark decocted in milk stops diarrhea and soothes intestinal irritation. Salve made with resin is used to heal wounds and persistent skin rashes.

HARVESTING: Collect resin from naturally occurring or intentional incisions in the bark of the sweet gum tree. Look for honey-colored resin beads on the bark. The best time to harvest resin is during warm weather just as the leaves are emerging, but you may collect the sweet gum resin anytime it appears. It is often necessary to return to the same trees every few days to collect enough resin. Use a knife and scrape resin carefully, taking care not to damage the tree's bark. Store resin in a small jar until needed.

Collect bark in the spring. Trim thick branches from the tree, strip and discard leaves, and use a sharp knife to scrape off the outer bark. Gather leaves in spring or early summer.

 # Sweet Gum Salve

Sweet gum resin, like many medicinal resins, is a powerful antiseptic that effectively heals infected wounds, relieves itching, and promotes healing. Making the salve requires several steps.

First, collect about two to three tablespoons of sweet gum resin. Then, make a simple tincture by steeping the resin in undiluted grain alcohol for several weeks, using one part resin (by weight) to two parts grain alcohol (by volume). Most of the resin will dissolve in the alcohol. Strain out any lumps that remain.

Mix one part resin tincture with two parts olive oil. Cook mixture over a low heat, stirring occasionally, until all the alcohol has evaporated, leaving behind the resin-infused olive oil. Use this oil to make a standard salve.[60]

Apply salve as needed to the skin.

PREPARATIONS:

- ◊ DECOCTION: Use one-half cup dried strips of the inner bark or one cup fresh leaves to one quart of water. Cover and simmer for 30 minutes. Strain and sweeten if desired.

- ◊ MILK TEA: Slowly cook one tablespoon dried bark or five or six chopped fresh leaves in milk over a low heat for 15 to 20 minutes, stirring often. Strain and sweeten with honey.

DOSAGES:

- ◊ DECOCTION: Drink one-half cup of bark decoction two to three times a day.

- ◊ MILK TEA: Drink one-half cup warm tea every 30 minutes or as needed.

- ◊ RESIN: As needed, chew peanut-sized lumps of sweet gum resin to treat mouth sores or sore throat.

Sweetfern

COMMON NAME: Sweetfern

BOTANICAL NAME: *Comptonia peregrina*

FAMILY: *Myricaceae* (Wax Myrtle)

DESCRIPTION: Sweetfern is a small shrub, one to three feet tall, with a woody stem and fernlike appearance. Deep green, alternate leaves, lance-shaped with rounded teeth, appear late in the spring. When crushed, the leaves release a wonderful spicy fragrance. When in bloom at midsummer, the inconspicuous green flowers are easy to miss. In the fall, look for small burr-like fruits that contain aromatic nuts.
MPH: p. 284.

HABITAT: Dry, open areas, often in poor soil.

KEY ACTIONS: Astringent, alterative, carminative

PART USED: Leaf

TRADITIONAL USES: American Indians made frequent use of the delightfully aromatic leaves of sweetfern: they were crushed and inhaled to relieve headaches, burned in religious ceremonies for purification, and used to sprinkle water on fire-heated rocks to create steam. Strong infusions of the leaf are a traditional remedy to treat poison ivy.[61]

CURRENT USES: Though not available commercially, sweetfern enjoys a reputation as a reliable folk remedy. Easy to identify and prolific, sweetfern is an effective poison ivy remedy. Infusions are used to treat symptoms of sluggish digestion such as gas, nausea, and abdominal bloating. The tea is also useful in the treatment of acute diarrhea. Use strong decoctions as a wash to dry up poison ivy rash, cool sunburn, and reduce the inflammation of eruptive skin conditions such as acne. These same preparations are used as an astringent douche used to treat vaginal discharges or as a gargle to treat inflamed gums or sore throat.

HARVESTING: Harvest leaves in the early summer before they dry out from the heat. Larger leaves have stronger astringent properties and are best used for topical preparations. Smaller, younger leaves contain less tannin and are a better choice in teas for use internally. For the strongest aromatic properties, harvest sweetfern early in the day.

Harvest several leaves from each plant, leaving enough foliage for the plant to continue to grow. Leaves may be dried on a screen or loosely bundled and hung up to dry. Sweetfern dries easily even in humid weather. Crumble dry leaves and store in glass jars.

PREPARATIONS:

◆ DECOCTION: For external use, make a decoction using one-half cup dried or one cup fresh leaves for each quart of water. Bring to a boil; cover and simmer for 20 minutes. Strain and cool. Pour over affected area as often as needed.

◆ INFUSION: For internal use, make a cold infusion using one-half cup dried or one cup fresh chopped leaves for each quart of water. Use smaller leaves if possible and crush or crumble them first. Infuse the herb in cold water for several hours. Strain and sweeten if desired.

DOSAGES: Sweetfern is not recommended for long term use internally.

◗ DECOCTION: Use a cool wash, douche, or compress as often as needed. Gargle several times a day to relieve sore throat or gum inflammation.

◗ INFUSION: Drink one cup several times a day or as needed.

Turtlehead

COMMON NAME: Turtlehead

BOTANICAL NAME: *Chelone glabra*

FAMILY: *Scrophulariaceae* (Figwort)

OTHER NAMES: Balmony, snakehead, turtlebloom

DESCRIPTION: Turtlehead is an upright perennial, two to four feet tall. It has sessile opposite leaves that are lance-shaped with toothed edges and a square stem. Distinctive two-lipped pale pink or white flowers resemble the shape of a turtle's head. Flowers bloom from late summer into early autumn.
MPH: pp. 15-16.

HABITAT: Turtlehead is most common along waterways. It prefers moist, shaded areas and is usually found growing with cardinal flower (*Lobelia cardinalis*) and jewelweed (*Impatiens capensis*).

KEY ACTIONS: Hepatic, cholagogue, bitter stimulant, laxative, anti-inflammatory, anti-emetic, anti-helmintic, cathartic

PART USED: Aerial (in flower)

TRADITIONAL USES: American Indians used turtlehead to

stimulate the appetite, as a laxative, and to expel worms. Some tribes believed the herb had contraceptive properties.[62]

During the Civil War, turtlehead was used to treat "impure conditions of the blood" such as jaundice, hepatitis, and constipation. Small doses of infusion were used as a general digestive system tonic. Turtlehead was a specific remedy for indigestion, bloating, poor digestion, and constipation. Larger doses were used to expel worms. The leaves were also used topically to treat ulcers, breast inflammation, hemorrhoids, and other inflammatory skin conditions.

CURRENT USES: Turtlehead is an effective herb that is probably underused in North American herbal practice. It is widely used in Europe where it is known by the common name "balmony."

Turtlehead is effective in the treatment of liver complaints including poor digestion, gastric upset, bloating, constipation, and lethargy after meals. A specific remedy to relieve inflammation of the gallbladder, turtlehead is often included in treatments for jaundice and hepatitis. Small doses act as an appetite stimulant and general digestive system tonic.

As a fresh leaf poultice, turtlehead is used to treat painful inflammations, including tumors, ulcers, boils, hemorrhoids and breast pain. Dried or fresh leaves can also be included in salve preparations.

HARVESTING: Collect the aerial parts of the plant when the flowers begin to bloom in late summer. Process fresh herb for tincture or skin salve, or dry for future use. Turtlehead dries easily when hung in bundles in a dry place with good air circulation.

PREPARATIONS:

- ◊ TINCTURE: Fresh herb – 1:2. Dried herb – 1:5. Menstruum – 45% alcohol.

- ◊ INFUSION: Use two teaspoons dried or one tablespoon fresh turtlehead for each cup of water. Cover and infuse for 20 minutes. Strain.

- ◊ POULTICE: Prepare a poultice by pounding the fresh leaves in a mortar and pestle until juicy. Add a small amount of water or aloe vera gel if needed to hold leaves together.

- ◊ SALVE: Make a standard salve with infused oil of fresh or dried turtlehead herb.

DOSAGES: To reap the full medicinal benefits of turtlehead, the bitter flavor of the herb must register on the tongue. For this reason, the tincture or infusion should be held in the mouth for several seconds before swallowing. Do not sweeten it or add it to fruit juices. Large doses may have a laxative effect. Start with the lowest recommended dose and gradually increase if needed.

- ◊ TINCTURE: Take 10 to 30 drops in a small amount of warm water after meals to relieve indigestion and bloating. As a tonic, take 20 to 30 drops two or three times a day for several months.

- ◊ INFUSION: Drink one cup of warm infusion after meals to stimulate digestion. As a tonic, drink one cup of infusion twice a day for one month or longer.

- ◊ POULTICE: Apply as needed to relieve symptoms.

- ◊ SALVE: Apply as needed to relieve symptoms.

Virginia Snakeroot

COMMON NAME: Virginia Snakeroot

BOTANICAL NAME: *Aristolochia serpentaria*

FAMILY: *Aristolochiaceae* (Birthwort)

RELATED SPECIES: Dutchman's pipe (*A. macrophylla* or *A. tormentosa*)

DESCRIPTION: Virginia snakeroot is a perennial vine, one to two feet long, with heart-shaped leaves and unusual brownish purple flowers that are "S" shaped, like an old-fashioned pipe. Blooms appear near the ground at the base of the plant from May to July. The root smells like turpentine.

A related species, Dutchman's pipe (*A. macrophylla* or *A. tormentosa*), is a woody vine with large heart-shaped leaves and bigger, showier pipe-shaped flowers. Medicinal properties are similar to *A. serpentaria* but much milder.

MPH: pp. 251-252.

HABITAT: Cool, moist slopes in deciduous forests. Commonly found growing with maidenhair fern (*Adiantum pedatum*), blue cohosh (*Caulophyllum thalictroides*), and wild geranium (*Geranium maculatum*). Due to hundreds of years of over-harvesting, Virginia snakeroot is now rare.

KEY ACTIONS: Digestive system tonic, stimulant, diaphoretic, anti-inflammatory

PART USED: Root and rhizome

TRADITIONAL USES: American Indians used Virginia snake-root to treat a wide range of symptoms. As a remedy for snakebites, the fresh bruised root was applied directly on bites. Fresh roots were also used to relieve toothaches. It was used to relieve pain, especially sharp pains in the stomach or breast. Small doses of the infusion were taken to treat rheumatism, indigestion, fevers, general weakness, and as a gargle for sore throats.[63]

CURRENT USES: Virginia snakeroot is not readily available on the commercial herb market. It is a very strong medicine that causes an immediate physical reaction even when taken in small doses. Short term, cautious use of the tincture stimulates digestion and appetite. Drinking even small amounts of warm infusion may cause sweating. When taken in a large dose, it is a fast acting, reliable emetic.

HARVESTING: Dig roots and rhizomes in the fall just as the nights begin to cool but before frost kills the leaves. Process fresh or cut into small pieces to dry.

PREPARATIONS: Virginia snakeroot is rich in volatile oils and, unlike most other roots, should be infused.

  ♦ TINCTURE: Fresh or dried root- 1:10. Menstruum – 50% alcohol.

  ♦ INFUSION: Use one teaspoon dried or two teaspoons fresh root for each cup of water. Cover and steep for 15 minutes. Strain.

DOSAGES: Virginia snakeroot should not be used for more than a few days at a time. Small doses given throughout the day are most effective. Large doses can cause nausea and vomiting.

- TINCTURE: Take five to 10 drops three times a day or as needed for acute conditions.

- INFUSION: Drink one tablespoon of the infusion three times a day or as needed for acute conditions.

Wild Cherry

COMMON NAME: Wild Cherry

BOTANICAL NAME: *Prunus serotina*

FAMILY: *Rosaceae* (Rose)

OTHER NAMES: Black cherry, wild black cherry

RELATED SPECIES: Choke cherry (*Prunus virginiana*)

DESCRIPTION: Wild cherry is a deciduous tree, 50 to 80 feet tall, with distinctive dark shiny bark marked with horizontal raised lines. Oval leaves with sharply toothed edges are smooth on top while the undersides are pale with hair along the midrib. Small white flowers bloom between April and June in finger-sized racemes that hang down from the ends of branches. In late summer, look for dark blue-black berries with large seeds. The bark has a bitter almond smell.
    MPH: p. 327.

HABITAT: Common in wooded areas throughout the region.

KEY ACTIONS: Stimulating expectorant, anti-spasmodic, astringent, diaphoretic, sedative

PART USED: Bark, fruit

TRADITIONAL USES: Wild cherry bark is a time-honored remedy used by the Cherokee and other American Indians to relieve coughs, fevers, and sore throats. Wild cherry bark infusion was used as a uterine tonic and sedative at the onset of labor. Topically, the infusion was used as a wash for skin or eye irritation. Cooked berries were used as a remedy for acute diarrhea symptoms. Dried berries were mixed with animal fats to make pemmican, a winter food.[64]

CURRENT USES: Wild cherry bark acts as a stimulating expectorant for lung congestion and coughs. It relieves symptoms of inflammation and irritation caused by colds, bronchitis, and pneumonia; and also reduces fevers. Use to treat sore throats and dry, spasmodic coughs. Stimulates and improves digestion. Wild cherry soothes irritation of mucus membranes in the respiratory system, stomach and urinary tract. It has a sedating effect on the nerves and heart, making it an effective treatment of fevers, heart palpitations, and general weakness. It can be used as a mild sedative for restlessness and insomnia caused by cold symptoms.

Use a decoction as a wash to soothe skin and eye irritation.

HARVESTING: Collect bark in the fall after the first frost. The bark from thick branches of young trees is most potent. Cut bark from branches into long strips. Cut or chop the bark into small pieces. Pick berries when fully ripe, usually in late July. Cook berries and strain out the seeds before eating. Wild cherry leaves are toxic.

PREPARATIONS: Unlike most barks, wild cherry bark is made as a cold infusion for internal use. The decoction is recommended for external use as a wash.

Traditionally, wild cherry bark is made into a simple syrup, often with other lung herbs such as mullein (*Verbascum thapsus*)

Wild Cherry Cough Syrup

Some variation of this syrup, inspired by a recipe used by Tommie Bass, should be in every home before winter arrives. If you make this in August or September, most of the herbs can be easily gathered fresh.

3 oz. fresh or 6 oz. dried wild cherry bark
3 oz. fresh or 6 oz. dried sweet gum bark
2 bunches ripe, fresh sumac berries
1 oz. fresh or 2 oz. dried bloodroot
2 oz. fresh or 4 oz. dried black cohosh root
Approximately four cups of chopped, fresh herbs: any combination of boneset, goldenrod, rabbit tobacco, spicebush leaf, and/or sumac leaf.

Put the sweet gum bark in a pot with two quarts of water; cover and simmer for 20 minutes. Remove from heat; add all other herbs. Use a spoon to push all the herbs down into the water. Steep overnight. In the morning, strain out the herbs and discard.

Measure the herb mixture and place in a clean pot. Bring to a boil; reduce heat to a simmer and cover. Cook until the total volume is reduced by half (about one quart). While the decoction is still hot, stir in one pint of honey. Mix well. Pour into sterilized bottles and store in the refrigerator.

Take one to two tablespoons of syrup as needed for coughs and sore throat. The syrup may be added to hot tea. Use as often as needed to relieve symptoms.

Note that this recipe is open to endless variation depending on the herbs you have on hand. Other herbs to consider include coltsfoot, elder flowers, elderberries, elecampane, horehound, mullein, sage, and thyme. Feel free to experiment.

and boneset (*Eupatorium perfoliatum*), to treat coughs and lung congestion. A simple brandy tincture may be used as a sedative and to improve digestion.

- INFUSION: Use one-half ounce dried bark for each pint of cool water. Chop bark into small pieces and steep for three to four hours. Strain.

- DECOCTION: Use one teaspoon dried bark for each cup of water. Bring to a boil; cover and simmer for 15 minutes. Strain. (For external use only.)

- BRANDY FOLK TINCTURE: Fill a quart jar half full of dried cherry bark and add brandy to fill the jar. Cover and store in a cool, dark place for one week, shaking daily. Strain and discard the bark.

DOSAGES:

- INFUSION: Drink one cup three to four times a day or as needed.

- DECOCTION: As a wash for skin or eye irritation, use cool decoction as often as needed.

- BRANDY FOLK TINCTURE: Take one teaspoon after meals or as needed to relieve digestive discomfort or as a sedative.

Wild Geranium

COMMON NAME: Wild Geranium

BOTANICAL NAME: *Geranium maculatum*

FAMILY: *Geraniaceae* (Geranium)

OTHER NAMES: Cranesbill, alumroot, stork's bill, dove's foot, pigeon's foot, American tormentil

RELATED SPECIES: Carolina cranesbill (*G. carolinianum*), Herb Robert (*G. robertianum*)

DESCRIPTION: Wild geranium is a gangly perennial, one to two feet tall. The leaves are deeply cleft into three to five segments with rough-toothed edges along the tip. Delicate pinkish-purple flowers with five petals bloom between April and June. The seedpod, shaped like a long pointed beak, resembles a crane's bill.

Carolina cranesbill (*G. carolinianum*) is a slightly smaller plant with intricately cut leaves and toothed margins. Leaves grow in three segments. The central segment has a long stalk while the lower segments are paired and much smaller. Flowers are pinkish-purple, with all the petals fused at the base to form a short tube. The entire plant has a pungent aroma.

An introduced European species, Herb Robert (*G. robertianum*) is less common. Its medicinal use is the same as *G. maculatum*.

MPH: pp. 165-166.

HABITAT: Moist shaded areas throughout the region.

KEY ACTIONS: Astringent, styptic, anti-inflammatory

PART USED: Root, leaf

TRADITIONAL USES: Wild geranium is a powerful, all-purpose astringent with a long history of use by American Indians as an acute remedy for excessive bleeding, debilitating diarrhea, and excessive discharges anywhere in the body.

Wild geranium was the remedy given when everything else failed to relieve severely acute symptoms. Common uses include the treatment of thrush, canker sores, ulcers, vaginal discharge, diarrhea, and heavy menstrual bleeding.

CURRENT USES: Wild geranium is a fast-acting astringent remedy that reduces excessive discharges without causing symptoms of dryness. It is used internally and externally. Use tincture or water extract internally to treat bleeding ulcers, or severe diarrhea, and to reduce heavy menstrual flow. The fresh or dried plant simmered in milk is a remedy for diarrhea and gastritis. Frequent use as a gargle helps heal canker sores, cold sores, thrush, and sore throat. An infusion used as a douche will reduce vaginal discharge. An infusion or decoction used as a wash soothes skin inflammation or conjunctivitis. Use wild geranium in salves to help shrink hemorrhoids or treat skin infections. The dried powdered root placed directly into a wound stops bleeding.

HARVESTING: Collect fresh leaves anytime during the growing season to make infusions or use as a poultice. Dig wild geranium roots in mid summer after flowers have faded and seeds are ripe.

178

Clean the root, chop into small pieces, and dry completely. The root is considered the most potent part of the plant. The leaf is a slightly milder medicine.

PREPARATIONS: Like many other astringent herbs used to treat severe diarrhea, wild geranium is often simmered in milk to make a fast-acting, soothing remedy.

- TINCTURE: Fresh root – 1:2. Dried root – 1:5. Menstruum – 45% alcohol.

- INFUSION: Use one and a half teaspoons of dried leaf or one tablespoon fresh leaf, chopped or crushed, for each cup of water. Cover and steep for 10 to 15 minutes.

- DECOCTION: Use one teaspoon dried root for each cup of water. Bring to a boil; cover and simmer for 10 to 15 minutes. Strain.

- MILK TEA: Use one teaspoon dried root or two teaspoons dried leaf in one cup of milk. Slowly heat to a simmer; cook for 15 minutes, stirring frequently. Strain and sweeten. Drink while warm.

- SALVE: Make a salve using infused oil of geranium leaf and/or root.

DOSAGES: Use small frequent doses of wild geranium to bring acute symptoms under control.

- TINCTURE: Take 20 to 40 drops every hour or as needed to manage symptoms.

- INFUSION/DECOCTION: Drink one cup every hour or as needed. As a gargle or wash, repeat treatment three times a day.

- MILK TEA: Drink one cup of warm tea every hour or as needed.
- SALVE: Use salve as often as needed.

Wild Ginger

COMMON NAME: Wild Ginger

BOTANICAL NAME: *Asarum canadense*

FAMILY: *Aristolochiaceae* (Birthwort)

RELATED SPECIES: Little brown jug (*Hexastylis arifolia*), heartleaf (*H. virginica*)

DESCRIPTION: Wild ginger is a low-growing deciduous perennial, four to five inches tall, with thick, glossy, kidney-shaped leaves, one on each stem. The solitary maroon-brown flower with a white interior lies on the ground at the base of the leaves. The flower is shaped like an upright bell with three long pointed lobes. It blooms April to May.

Two other members of the Birthwort family are often misidentified as *Asarum canadense*: little brown jug (*H. arifolia*) and heartleaf (*H. virginica*). Both have evergreen leaves and maroon-brown flowers that lie on the ground at the base of the leaves. *H. arifolia* has triangular leaves, and the flower lobes meet at the top, giving it a rounded shape that resembles a jug. *H. virginica* has rounded kidney-shaped leaves similar to wild ginger, but the flowers are larger with three exaggerated triangular lobes that are mottled maroon and white with a darker interior. *H. arifolia* and *H. virginica* are used interchangeably with wild ginger.[65]

MPH: pp. 155-156.

HABITAT: In the deep shade of deciduous forests.

KEY ACTIONS: Carminative, diaphoretic

PART USED: Root

TRADITIONAL USES: The Cherokee used wild ginger for a wide range of symptoms. It was taken internally to bring on delayed menses, relieve stomach and breast pain, lower fevers, and soothe coughs. Stronger preparations were used to induce vomiting, and to expel worms. Fresh leaf poultice or salve was applied to wounds. Dried root was used as a snuff for headaches and sinus congestion.[66]

Wild ginger has been used throughout the region as a mild folk remedy for stomach upset, colic, coughs, and delayed menses.

CURRENT USES: Wild ginger use is rare in modern herbal practice. Like many woodland natives, it is threatened by shrinking habitat. Root infusion is used to relieve an upset stomach, relieve menstrual cramps, or soothe coughs. Its actions are much milder than those of commercially grown tropical ginger (*Zingiber officinale*).

HARVESTING: Harvest the roots in the fall. Clean carefully; slice into small pieces and dry for future use.

PREPARATIONS:

◖ TINCTURE: Fresh root – 1:2. Dried root – 1:5. Menstruum – 50% alcohol.

◖ INFUSION: Use one teaspoon dried or two teaspoons fresh root for each cup of water. Cover and steep for 30 minutes. Strain.

DOSAGES: Wild ginger is not for long term use. Large or frequent doses may cause nausea.

- TINCTURE: Take 20 to 30 drops in a small amount of warm water every half-hour or as needed to relieve symptoms.

- INFUSION: Drink one or two tablespoons of warm decoction every half-hour or as needed to relieve symptoms.

Wild Hydrangea

COMMON NAME: Wild Hydrangea

BOTANICAL NAME: *Hydrangea arborescens*

FAMILY: *Saxifragaceae* (Saxifrage)

OTHER NAMES: Sevenbark

DESCRIPTION: Wild hydrangea is a shrub, four to six feet tall, with opposite, paired leaves that are oval and sharply pointed with serrated edges. Tiny white flowers grow in round clusters. Irregularly lobed, sterile flowers with papery, white petals surround the true flowers in the central clusters. Wild hydrangea blooms between June and August. The bark has a peeled appearance, curling back in thin layers along the stem.
MPH: p. 273.

HABITAT: Common understory shrub in deciduous forests.

KEY ACTIONS: Diuretic, anti-lithic, analgesic

PART USED: Root bark

TRADITIONAL USES: American Indians used wild hydrangea root bark as a poultice for burns, ulcers, and rashes. The bark was chewed to relieve high blood pressure and stomach problems. In folk medicine, wild hydrangea was used extensively to treat kidney problems including blood in the urine, kidney stones and infections.[67] Herbalist Tommie Bass relied heavily on wild hydrangea to treat gallbladder problems, kidney stones, rheumatic inflammation, gout, and liver congestion.[68]

CURRENT USES: Wild hydrangea is an effective treatment for the acute symptoms of kidney and bladder problems including cystitis, kidney stones, and enlarged or inflamed prostate. It also relieves pain associated with acute urinary tract problems, including lower back pain and painful urination.

HARVESTING: Dig the roots in late summer or early autumn after the flowers have bloomed. Wash the roots and remove the outer bark by scraping it with a sharp knife. Immediately cut the root into small pieces.

PREPARATIONS: Combine with other kidney herbs to address specific symptoms. For prostatitis, combine with horsetail (*Equisetum arvense*). For kidney stones, combine with Joe-pye-weed (*Eupatorium purpureum*) and pipsissewa (*Chimaphila maculatum*).

● TINCTURE: Fresh root – 1:2. Dried root – 1:5. Menstruum – 45% alcohol.

● DECOCTION: Use one teaspoon dried root or two teaspoons fresh root for each cup of water. Bring to a boil; cover and simmer for 20 minutes. Strain.

DOSAGE: Any acute symptoms listed above may indicate a kidney infection, especially when accompanied by sharp pain and fever. A kidney infection is life-threatening. If these symptoms occur, immediately seek an accurate diagnosis, from a medical pro-

185

fessional trained to diagnose acute kidney infections, before attempting to treat with herbs.

- TINCTURE: Take 30 to 50 drops of tincture in a small amount of water three to four times a day. Increase dosage, up to two teaspoons of tincture per dose, if needed.

- DECOCTION: Drink three cups of warm decoction every two to three hours or as needed.

Wild Yam

COMMON NAME: Wild Yam

BOTANICAL NAME: *Dioscorea villosa*

FAMILY: *Dioscoreaceae* (Yam)

OTHER NAMES: Colic root, rheumatism root

RELATED SPECIES: *D. quaternata*

DESCRIPTION: Wild yam is a non-woody, perennial vine. The heart-shaped leaves have distinctive, parallel veins that run evenly from leaf axis almost to the tip. Small, inconspicuous, green flowers bloom from May to July, followed in the fall by small triangular seed capsules. The plant starts out upright with the first few leaves in whorls of four to eight. As the twining, smooth vine continues to grow from the center of the whorl, its leaves are alternate. Wild yam vines can reach lengths of 15 feet.
   MPH: pp. 230-231

HABITAT: Common in deciduous woods.

KEY ACTIONS: Anti-inflammatory, anti-spasmodic, cholagogue

PART USED: Root

TRADITIONAL USES: American Indians used wild yam to help relieve labor pains. It is a traditional folk remedy for colic, intestinal cramps, morning sickness and pain from arthritis and rheumatism.

CURRENT USES: Wild yam is an important medicine in modern herbal practice. It is a fast-acting remedy for pain, cramps and inflammation anywhere in the body. Small, frequent doses relieve spasms caused by Irritable Bowel Syndrome, diverticulitis, and colic. It is a specific remedy for relieving menstrual cramps. Wild yam also reduces inflammation caused by rheumatoid arthritis, helps settle the stomach, and eases morning sickness.

HARVESTING: Dig roots in the fall. Clean carefully and use strong clippers to immediately cut into very small pieces. Once wild yam root dries, it is as hard as stone and almost impossible to cut or grind.

PREPARATIONS: All wild yam preparations are made with dried root.

◊ TINCTURE: Dried root – 1:5. Menstruum – 50% alcohol.

◊ DECOCTION: Use one to two teaspoons of dried root for each cup of water. Bring water to a boil; simmer for 15 to 20 minutes. Strain.

DOSAGES: Use wild yam in small, frequent doses until symptoms improve. Wait about 30 minutes between doses. As symptoms improve, increase the time between doses.

- TINCTURE: Take 20 to 40 drops every 30 minutes or as need-ed to relieve symptoms.

- DECOCTION: Drink one cup of decoction every 30 minutes or as needed to relieve symptoms.

Witch Hazel

COMMON NAME: Witch Hazel

BOTANICAL NAME: *Hamamelis virginiana*

FAMILY: *Hamamelidaceae* (Witch Hazel)

DESCRIPTION: Witch hazel is a small deciduous tree, 10 to 12 feet tall, with alternate ovate leaves that widen slightly near the tips. Leaf edges are wavy. Delicate small yellow flowers, with four narrow petals that resemble thin shreds of crepe paper, bloom between October and December, after the leaves have all fallen.
MPH: pp. 287-288.

HABITAT: Deciduous forests. Witch hazel is often abundant in transition zones at the edge of forests, in open sunny areas, and along waterways.

KEY ACTIONS: Astringent, anti-inflammatory

PART USED: Leaf, bark

TRADITIONAL USES: The Cherokee rubbed the fresh leaves on the skin to treat scratches, and used an infusion of the leaves as a wash for sores and skin abrasions. Witch hazel decoction was taken internally to relieve menstrual pain, fever, sore throats, and diarrhea.[69]

Witch Hazel - Hamamelis virginiana

Distilled witch hazel, a time-tested home remedy, has been a staple in North American medicine chests for several hundred years. It has been used widely as a treatment for the pain and inflammation of varicose veins, sprains, bruises, cuts, abrasions, hemorrhoids, smashed fingers and toes, shaving rash, and insect bites.

Dowsers have traditionally used the forked branch of a witch hazel tree to locate underground water.

CURRENT USES: Witch hazel is a reliable remedy that deserves a place in every first aid kit. Witch hazel infusion or tincture is used internally to control severe diarrhea and reduce excessive menstrual bleeding. The infusion is used as a wash for the eyes and as a gargle for sore throat. Cotton balls or gauze saturated with witch hazel (distilled or liniment) offer immediate relief for hemorrhoids, burns, varicose veins, bug bites, sprains, sore muscles, backaches, and bruises.

HARVESTING: Collect leaves, bark and twigs anytime in the spring and early summer. Cut branches, strip off leaves, and use a knife to peel off the outer bark. Fresh bark and branches less than one-half inch in diameter can be chopped into small pieces. Strip leaves off of branches.

PREPARATIONS: Although distilled witch hazel is readily available, an effective home remedy can be made for topical applications by steeping fresh leaves and bark in rubbing alcohol. Commercially distilled witch hazel is a high-potency alcohol extract intended for external use only.

When making witch hazel tincture, vegetable glycerin is added to the menstruum to better extract the tannins.

- **FRESH BARK TINCTURE:** Fresh bark and leaf – 1:2. Menstruum – 65% alcohol and 10% vegetable glycerin.

- **DRIED BARK TINCTURE:** Dried bark and leaf – 1:5. Menstruum – 50% alcohol and 10% vegetable glycerin.

- **INFUSION:** Use one teaspoon dried or two teaspoons fresh leaves, chopped twigs, or bark for each cup of water. Cover and steep for 15 minutes. Strain.

- **LINIMENT:** Fill a quart jar with fresh crushed leaves and chopped bark and twigs. Pour in enough rubbing alcohol to cover herb completely. Steep for two weeks and shake the jar daily. Strain and label: For External Use Only.

DOSAGES: For external use, witch hazel infusion and liniment can be used interchangeably with commercially distilled witch hazel. All three preparations are excellent astringents for relieving inflammation.

- **TINCTURE:** Take 10 drops of tincture two to three times a day.

- **INFUSION:** Drink one cup two to three times a day. The infusion is also used as a compress, wash, or douche as needed.

- **LINIMENT:** Soak cotton balls or gauze in liniment and apply to the skin to treat sore muscles. Do not use liniment on broken skin.

Yellowroot

COMMON NAME: Yellowroot

BOTANICAL NAME: *Xanthorhiza simplicissima*

FAMILY: *Ranunculaceae* (Buttercup)

OTHER NAMES: Redneck goldenseal

DESCRIPTION: Yellowroot is a woody perennial, one to three feet tall, with five leaves composed of deeply-cleft, toothed leaflets on each stalk. The brown outer bark of the main stems easily peels away to reveal a bright-yellow inner bark. Just below the leaves, small star-shaped greenish-brown flowers are arranged in a drooping spray. As the season progresses, the flowers slowly turn a dark brown-maroon color. Look for blooms April to August. The yellow roots are woody and fibrous and have an acrid smell.

HABITAT: Grows in dense thickets along streambeds and other wet shady areas. Yellowroot is endemic to the southern Appalachian mountains.

KEY ACTIONS: Digestive bitter, hepatic, antiseptic, anti-fungal

PART USED: Root

TRADITIONAL USES: Yellowroot was used by the Cherokee to

treat jaundice, hepatitis, and chronic liver problems, and to heal persistent ulcers. It was also used as a dye for baskets.[70]

In Southern folk medicine, yellowroot was considered a general tonic to improve overall health and a remedy for indigestion, ulcers, and heartburn. The root was decocted to make a wash used to treat sties, thrush, gum disease, toothaches, and skin rashes.

CURRENT USES: Yellowroot has actions similar to goldenseal (*Hydrastis canadensis*), though it is a much milder medicine. It is used as a bitter tonic to improve digestion and elimination. Yellow root is a specific remedy for healing gastric ulcers.

Yellowroot decoction is used as a wash to clean wounds; as a gargle and mouthwash for sore throats, thrush, and bleeding gums; and as a nasal flush for sinus infections. The salve is used for bedsores, persistent ulcers, fungal infections, and general wound healing.

HARVESTING: Dig roots in the spring just as the flowers and leaves appear, or in the fall around the time of the first frost. Clean the root carefully and immediately cut into one-inch pieces.

PREPARATIONS:

 ◆ TINCTURE: Fresh root – 1:2. Dried root – 1:5. Menstruum – 65% alcohol.

 ◆ DECOCTION: Use one-half teaspoon dried or one teaspoon fresh root for each cup of water. Bring to a boil; cover and simmer for 20 minutes. Strain.

 ◆ SALVE: Make a salve using infused yellowroot oil.

Notes

[1]Thoreau, *The Heart of Thoreau's Journals*, 99.
[2]Moerman, *Native American Ethnobotany*, 162-163.
[3]Wiggington and Bennett, *Foxfire 9*, 132.
[4]Porcher, *Resources of Southern Fields and Forests*, 155.
[5]Crellin and Philpott, *A Reference Guide to Medicinal Plants*, 102.
[6]Patton, *Tommie Bass: Herb Doctor of Shinbone Ridge*, 103.
[7]Crellin and Philpott, *A Reference Guide to Medicinal Plants*, 102.
[8]Crellin and Philpott, 106.
[9]Moerman, *Native American Ethnobotany*, 83.
[10]Patton, *Tommie Bass: Herb Doctor of Shinbone Ridge*, 126.
[11]Moerman, *Native American Ethnobotany*, 511.
[12]Moerman, 361.
[13]Kuhn and Winston, *Herbal Therapies and Supplements*, 124.
[14]Moore, *Medicinal Plants of the Mountain West*, 75.
[15]Moerman, *Native American Ethnobotany*, 158.
[16]Crellin and Philpott, *A Reference Guide to Medicinal Plants*, 218.
[17]Hobbs, *Foundations of Health*, 233.
[18]Felter and Lloyd, *King's American Dispensatory*, 925.
[19]Foster and Chongxi, *Herbal Emissaries*, 105.
[20]Moerman, *Native American Ethnobotany*, 376.
[21]Foster and Chongxi, *Herbal Emissaries*, 106-107.
[22]Moerman, *Native American Ethnobotany*, 536-537.
[23]Crellin and Philpott, *A Reference Guide to Medicinal Plants*, 231.
[24]Winston, "Nvwote: Cherokee Medicine and Ethnobotany,"
    American Herbalism, 94-95.
[25]Moerman, *Native American Ethnobotany*, 274.
[26]Foster and Duke, *A Field Guide to Medicinal Plants and Herbs*, 184-185.
[27]Martin, *Wildflower Folklore*, 26.
[28]Winston, David, personal communication, 2003.
[29]Crellin and Philpott, *A Reference Guide to Medicinal Plants*, 274-276.
[30]Bergner, "Is Lobelia Toxic?" *Medical Herbalism*, Volume 10, No. 1 & 2,
    pp. 1, 15-17.

[31]Moerman, *Native American Ethnobotany*, 311-312.

[32]Porcher, *Resources of Southern Fields and Forests*, 401.

[33]Bergner and Treasure, "The Lost Forms of Lobelia," *Medical Herbalism*, Vol. 10, No. 1 & 2, pp. 33-34.

[34]Duke, James A., "A Pointer Weed?" *Wild Foods Forum*. Volume 14, No. 1, pp. 8-10.

[35]Moerman, *Native American Ethnobotany*, 50.

[36]Krochmal, Walters, Doughty, *Medicinal Plants of Appalachia*, 34.

[37]Moore, *Medicinal Plants of the Mountain West*, 100.

[38]Moerman, *Native American Ethnobotany*, 456.

[39]Crellin and Philpott, *A Reference Guide to Medicinal Plants*, 251-252.

[40]Moerman, *Native American Ethnobotany*, 345.

[41]Crellin and Philpott, *A Reference Guide to Medicinal Plants*, 412-413.

[42]Moerman, *Native American Ethnobotany*, 379.

[43]Moerman, 157-158.

[44]Moerman, 250.

[45]Crellin and Philpott, *A Reference Guide to Medicinal Plants*, 365.

[46]Moerman, *Native American Ethnobotany*, 146.

[47]Crellin and Philpott, *A Reference Guide to Medicinal Plants*, 370-371.

[48]Moerman, *Native American Ethnobotany*, 181-182.

[49]Moerman, 519-520.

[50]Moerman, 524.

[51]Moerman, 422.

[52]Moerman, 308.

[53]Moerman, 171.

[54]Moerman, 471-473.

[55]Patton, *Tommie Bass: Herb Doctor of Shinbone Ridge*, 135.

[56]Porcher, *Resources of Southern Fields and Forests*, 202.

[57]Moerman, *Native American Ethnobotany*, 309.

[58]Porcher, *Resources of Southern Fields and Forests*, 9.

[59]Patton, *Tommie Bass: Herb Doctor of Shinbone Ridge*, 309.

[60]Klein, Robyn, personal communication, 2002.

[61]Moerman, *Native American Ethnobotany*, 172.

[62]Moerman, 154.

[63]Moerman, 91-92.

[64]Moerman, 441-442.

[65]Crellin and Philpott, *A Reference Guide to Medicinal Plants*, 452-453.

[66]Moerman, *Native American Ethnobotany*, 105.

Notes

67Moerman, 270.
68Crellin and Philpott, *A Reference Guide to Medicinal Plants*, 392.
69Moerman, *Native American Ethnobotany*, 255.
70Moerman, 602.

Glossary

Acute. A symptom that appears suddenly and resolves itself in a fairly short time.

Adaptogen. A non-specific action that increases overall ability to respond and adapt to physical and mental stress.

Aerial. All of the parts of a plant that are above ground; i.e. stem, leaves, flowers, seeds or fruits.

Alkaloid. A chemical that contains nitrogen as part of a hetero-cyclic ring structure, usually with a strong physiological effect.

Alterative. General term used to describe the action of certain herbs to increase the efficiency of lymphatic system, kidneys, liver, and skin.

Alternate (leaves). Single leaves that grow on alternate sides along the stem.

Amenorrhea. Lack of menses.

Analgesic. Relieves pain.

Annual. A plant that lives for only one growing season.

Anodyne. Relieves pain symptoms and may affect consciousness.

Anther. The part of the stamen that produces pollen.

Anti-helmintic. Kills and/or purges worms or parasites.

Anti-bacterial. Kills or inhibits the growth of bacteria.

Anti-catarrhal. Reduces inflammation and congestion of mucus membranes.

Anti-depressant. Relieves symptoms of depression.

Anti-emetic. Prevents or relieves vomiting.

Anti-inflammatory. Relieves inflammation symptoms.

Anti-fungal. Kills fungi.

Anti-lithic. Breaks ups stones, or calculi, in the gallbladder or kidney. *See also* lithotropic.

Anti-microbial. Kills micro-organisms.

Antiseptic. Prevents or stops the growth of microrganisms.

Anti-spasmodic. Relieves muscle spasms and tightness.

Anti-tussive. Reduces coughing.

Anti-pyretic. Reduces fever.

Anti-rheumatic. Relieves rheumatic pain and inflammation.

Aromatic. Contains high amounts of volatile oils. *See also* carminative and diaphoretic.

Asthma. Obstruction of the airways caused by spasms of the bronchi.

Attention Deficit Disorder (ADD). Poor attention span and inappropriate, impulsive behavior. *See also* Attention Deficit/Hyperactivity Disorder.

Attention Deficit/Hyperactivity Disorder (ADHD). Same as ADD but with hyperactive physical behavior.

Axil. The angle formed at the point where a leaf attaches to the stem.

Basal. Leaves crowded around the base of the stem.

Basal rosette. Describes the way basal leaves look when many of them are crowded together at the base of the plant.

Bell's palsy. Weakness or paralysis of a facial nerve, usually occurring on only one side of the face. Cause is unknown but may be the result of viral infection, immune disorder, or Lyme's disease.

Biennial. Plants with a two-year growing cycle; first year's growth is limited to roots and leaves. During the second year, the plant produces flowers and seeds.

Bitter. Taste or flavor that stimulates bile and other secretions.

Bisexual (flowers). Flowers composed of both pistils and stamens.

Bract. Very small or modified leaf that appears near a flower.

Bronchitis. Inflammation of the bronchial tubes.

Cambium. Inner layer of a woody branch: a tube-like tissue that conducts fluids and nutrients from the roots to the leaves.

Candidiasis. Systemic fungal infection caused by *Candida albicans*.

Canker Sore. Ulcers on the mucus membranes in the mouth.

Cardiotonic. Regulates and strengthens heart function.

Carminative. Stimulates digestion; relieves flatulence, spasms, and bloating.

Catkin. A dangling spike of pistillate (lacking stamens) or staminate (lacking pistils) flowers that hangs off the branches of certain trees. Wind-pollinated.

Cathartic. Causes a dramatic evacuation of the large intestine. Usually acts as an irritant.

Cholagogue. Stimulates bile secretions from the gallbladder.

Chlorophyll. Green pigment in plants that indicates photosynthesis.

Circulatory stimulant. Increases blood circulation; may increase heart rate.

Cold Sore. Sore on the lip or mouth caused by the herpes simplex virus.

Colic. Abdominal contractions and pain, symptoms include nausea and vomiting.

Conjunctivitis. Bacterial or viral infection of the conjunctiva, or lining of the eyelid, that causes inflammation, discharge, and irritation. Contagious.

Compound (leaf). Leaflets arranged in distinct segments, attached to the stem at a common point, with one single leaf at the terminal end.

Compress. Herbal treatment that consists of a cloth saturated with a hot or cold herbal infusion or decoction that is applied to the skin. Used to relieve pain, congestion, inflammation, infection and other symptoms.

Contraindicated. Not to be used when specific symptoms are present.

Cystitis. Bladder infection.

Deciduous. Loses its leaves at the end of the growing season, in some cases when the leaves wither and dry up but remain on the plant.

Deciduous forest. A forest dominated by trees that lose their leaves at the end of the growing season.

Decoction. A water-based herbal extract made by boiling or simmering herbs in water for a specific amount of time.

Deep immune activator. Increases immune response; stimulates production of blood, T-cells, phagocytes, and other immune activity. Long term use strengthens immune response.

Demulcent. Soothes irritated internal tissues.

Diabetes. Abnormally high blood sugar levels caused by low levels of insulin.

Diaphoretic. Induces sweating; reduces or relieves fevers.

Diuretic. Stimulates urine production.

Diverticulitis. Inflammation of the diverticula or sac-like pockets in the large intestine.

Dysentery. Intestinal inflammation with varying causes. Symptoms include abdominal pain, cramping, and diarrhea.

Eclectic (physician). Physician from a school of medicine that flourished in the United States in the late 19th and early 20th centuries, and that researched and promoted medicinal plants native to North America.

Edema. Excessive fluid in the tissues caused by excessive sodium in the body. Causes swelling of the legs and feet. Also known as dropsy.

Emetic. Induces vomiting.

Emmenagogue. Stimulates menses; may be abortifacient in large doses.

Emollient. Soothing and moistening to external tissues.

Endemic (plant). A plant only found growing within a specific region.

Endometriosis. Disorder characterized by the appearance of endometrial tissues, normally found in the lining of the uterus, in other parts of the pelvis. Symptoms include severe cyclical pain, excessive menstrual bleeding, and infertility.

Escharotic. Folk remedy for the treatment of cancerous tumors, usually in the form a salve, applied topically to draw tumors to the surface of the skin.

Ethnobotany. Study of how plants are used by a specific group of people.

Evergreen. Leaves remain on the plant throughout all or most of the year.

Expectorant. Increases elimination of mucus from the lungs.

Febrifuge. Reduces fever. *See also* diaphoretic.

Fibromyalgia. A group of disorders characterized by symptoms that may include pain and stiffness throughout the body, poor sleep, fatigue, depression, and Irritable Bowel Syndrome.

Fistula, anal. A crack or fissure in the mucus membrane of the anus.

Flu. Influenza.

Folk method. Simple method of preparing herbal tinctures that involves macerating herbs in 80 or 100 proof alcohol and requires no measuring or weighing of ingredients.

Frond. The leaf of a fern.

Fibrocystic Breast Disease. Disease of the breast with symptoms that include pain and non-cancerous lumps and cysts.

Galactagogue. Increases the flow of breast milk.

Gastritis. Inflammation of the stomach lining. May lead to infections and/or peptic ulcers.

Gout. A disorder caused by deposits of crystals (sodium urate) in the joints as a result of high levels of uric acid in the blood. Symptoms include joint pain and inflammation, usually in the feet.

Hemorrhoids. Dilated or inflamed veins in the rectum or anus.

Hepatic. Tonifies and detoxifies the liver.

Hepatitis. Inflammation of the liver caused by the hepatitis virus, alcoholism, or pharmaceutical drug use.

Hormonal balancer. Nourishes the endocrine system, helps regulate hormonal secretions.

Hypnotic. Powerful sedative, depresses heart rate and respiration, causes sleepiness.

Hypotensive. Reduces blood pressure.

Indigenous. Native to the local area.

Influenza. An acute disease caused by viral infection of the respiratory tract. Contagious. Also referred to as the flu.

Infusion. Tea or water extract made by steeping fresh or dried herbs in hot or cold water for a specific period of time.

Inhalation. Herbal steam used to treat the respiratory system. Made by steeping herbs in boiling hot water and inhaling the steam.

Interstitial cystitis. Painful inflammation or ulceration of the bladder with no evidence of infection. Cause unknown.

Irritable Bowel Syndrome. A disorder that causes abdominal pain, cramping and explosive diarrhea, sometimes alternating with constipation. Possible causes include food allergies, stress, overeating, eating too quickly, and fatty foods.

Jaundice. Abnormally high levels of bilirubin the body. Symptoms include yellowing of the skin and eyes.

Labor tonic. An herbal preparation used during the last three weeks of pregnancy to prepare for childbirth. Also known as a parturient.

Laxative. Stimulates large intestine.

Lithotropic. Breaks up stones (calculi) in the kidney or gallbladder; may prevent recurrence.

Lymphatic. Stimulates lymphatic drainage, reduces swelling of the lymph nodes.

Leaf nodes. Points along a stem where leaves or leaf buds emerge.

Leaflet. Leaf segments that together form a compound leaf.

Leucorrhea. Vaginal discharge.

Lobed. Leaf margin with a rounded shape, like an ear lobe.

Macerate. To soften. The process of steeping a plant in a menstruum, or solvent, to extract active compounds.

Marc. The spent plant matter that remains after a tincture is pressed. The marc is of no medicinal value.

Menstruum. A liquid solvent used to make a tincture. Usually a combination of alcohol and water.

Mucolytic. Dissolves mucus, primarily in the respiratory system.

Naturalized. An introduced plant that is now well established and common in the area.

Naturopathic. System of natural healing that does not rely on drugs or surgery. Instead, it uses herbs, vitamins, hydrotherapy, and other healing techniques.

Nervine. Herb that strengthens, relaxes or stimulates the nervous system.

Opposite (leaves). Grow in pairs opposite from each other along the stem.

Oxalic acid. Ethanedioic acid, found in many plants and vegetables, toxic in large amounts.

Oxytocic. Stimulates uterine contractions; promotes labor (parturition).

Palmate. Shaped like the palm of the hand.

Panacea. Cure-all.

Partus preparator. A substance that readies the body for labor and childbirth.

Perennial. A plant with a growth cycle of three or more growing seasons.

Peripheral vasodilator. Expands peripheral blood vessels, increases blood circulation. May reduce blood pressure.

Pertussis. Bacterial infection of the air passages that causes inflammation and spasms of coughing that end in a loud whooping inhalation. Highly contagious. Also known as whooping cough.

Petiole. The stalk of a leaf.

***Petit mal* seizures**. Short epileptic seizures. Symptoms include fluttering eyelids, facial spasms and brief loss of consciousness (two to three seconds.)

Pinnate (leaf). Three or more leaflets arranged in two rows along a stalk

Pistil. Female reproductive organ of the flower. Consists of the stigma that receives the pollen, and the style: a tube-like structure that connects the stigma to the ovaries that contain the ovules (seeds.)

Pith. The soft center of a woody branch, found beneath the bark and cambium layers.

Pleurisy. Inflammation of the membrane surrounding the lung (pleura), often the result of pneumonia or other lung disease.

Pollinator. An insect or animal that visits flowers for nectar and in the process of moving from flower to flower, distributes pollen to cause fertilization.

Post-partum. Occurring after childbirth.

Poultice. A soft mass of fresh or dried herbs, moistened and applied to the skin to promote cellular healing, increase circulation, or treat pain and infections.

Prostatitis. Inflammation of the prostate gland caused by bacterial infection. Symptoms include painful or difficult urination.

Psoriasis. Chronic, scaly skin condition with inflammation and itching, sometimes caused by anxiety.

Pulmonary edema. Accumulation of fluid in the lungs with breathing difficulties. Caused by cardiac weakness.

Purgative. Causes dramatic evacuation of the bowels. *See also* cathartic.

Raceme. Flowers growing singly along a stem, sometimes described as a flower spike.

Radical (rosette). Leaves growing out from one point at the base of the plant. May also be referred to as a rosette.

Resin. Aromatic sap produced by trees as protection if the bark is damaged or cut.

Rheumatism. Disease of the joints. Symptoms include inflammation, pain and eventual destruction of the joints.

Rhinitis. Inflammation of the nose. Usually causes mucus discharge.

Rhizome. Underground plant stem that usually grows horizontally just below the surface of the ground and consists of leaf nodes with rootlets along its length. Also known as rootstock.

Rootlet. Small root.

Rootstock. Rhizome.

Rubefacient. Increases blood circulation by causing localized skin irritation. Used externally.

Salve. Medicinal preparation made from vegetable oil infused with herbs and thickened with beeswax, used topically.

Saprophytic. Plant that lives on dead or decaying organic matter.

Sciatica. Inflammation of the sciatic nerve that causes pain or numbness in the leg.

Sedative. Slows heart and respiratory rates. May reduce nervousness and anxiety.

Sepals. The outer parts of the flower envelope, usually green.

Serrated (leaf). Sharply toothed edges that point upward toward the leaf tip.

Sessile. A leaf that is attached directly to the stem, without a petiole.

Sialagogue. Stimulates the production of saliva, may increase appetite and improve digestion.

Simple (leaf). A single leaf growing directly from the stem.

Stamen. Male reproductive organs of a flower. Consists of the filament and the pollen-producing anther.

Stigma. Part of pistil or female reproductive organ of the flower located at the terminal end of the pistil. The stigma receives the pollen grains.

Stomachic. Stimulates the stomach, promotes the appetite and digestion. *See also* carminative and aromatic.

Styptic. Stops blood flow from wounds. Used externally.

Surface immune activator. Increases defensive responses of the skin and mucus membranes against invading pathogens.

Syrup. A sweet preparation usually made by combining a concentrated herbal decoction with honey or sugar.

Taproot. A long root that grows vertically into the ground, like a carrot.

Terminal. Growing at the end of a stem.

Thrush. Fungal infection of the mouth.

Tincture. A medicinal extract made by steeping plants in a combination of alcohol and water.

Tonic. An herb that has restorative properties, used to strengthen organ function and increase energy.

Umbel. A cluster of flowers on stalks that all radiate out from the same point. Viewed from below, the stalks and underside of the flower cluster resemble an umbrella.

Understory plants. Plants that thrive in shade produced by deciduous forests. Usually includes shrubs, seedlings and small trees.

Urethra. The channel that carries urine from the bladder out of the body.

Urethritis. Inflammation of the urethra.

Uterine tonic. Tonifies and strengthens the uterus. May increase capacity for conception.

Vaginitis. Inflammation of the vagina.

Vermifuge. Kills and purges parasites.

Vulnerary. Promotes tissue healing by stimulating cell regeneration, internal or external.

Whorled (leaves). Three or more leaves growing in a circle around one point on the stem.

Whooping cough. Bacterial infection of the air passages that causes inflammation and spasms of coughing that end in a loud whooping inhalation. Highly contagious. Also known as pertussis.

Bibliography

Adams, Kevin, and Marty Casstevens. *Wildflowers of the Southern Appalachians: How to Photograph and Identify Them.* Winston-Salem, N.C.: John F. Blair, Publisher. 1996.

Armitage, Alan M. *Herbaceous Perennial Plants.* Champaign, Il.: Stipes Publishing. 1989. Second edition. 1997.

Bensky, Dan, and Andrew Gamble with Ted Kaptchuk. *Chinese Herbal Medicine: Materia Medica.* Seattle, Wa.: Eastland Press. 1986.

Bergner, Paul "Is Lobelia Toxic?" *Medical Herbalism*, Volume 10, No. 1 & 2. Spring and Summer, 1998.

Bergner, Paul and Jonathan Treasure. "The Lost Forms of Lobelia." *Medical Herbalism* Volume 10, No. 1 & 2. Spring and Summer, 1998.

Brill, Steve "Wildman" with Evelyn Dean. *Identifying and Harvesting Edible and Medicinal Plants in Wild (and Not So Wild) Places.* New York: Hearst Books, William Morrow and Co., Inc. 1994.

Brinker, Frances. *Herb Contraindications and Drug Interactions.* Sandy, Or.: Eclectic Medical Publications. 1998.

British Herbal Medicine Association, Scientific Committee. *British Herbal Pharmacopoeia.* London: British Herbal Medicine Association. 1983.

Brown, O. Phelps. *The Complete Herbalist, or, The People Their Own Physicians.* Jersey City, N.J.: published by the author. 1897.

Cavender, Anthony. *Folk Medicine of Southern Appalachia.* Chapel Hill, N.C.: University of North Carolina Press. 2003.

Cech, Richo. *Making Plant Medicine.* Williams, Or.: Horizon Herbs Publications. 2000.

Cook, William H. *The Physio-Medical Dispensatory: A Treatise on Therapeutics, Materia Medica, and Pharmacy.* 1869. Reprint edition. Portland, Or.: Eclectic Medical Publications. 1985.

Couplan, Francois. *The Encyclopedia of Edible Wild Plants of North America: Nature's Green Feast.* New Canaan, Ct.: Keats Publishing. 1998.

Crellin, James A., and Jane Philpott. *A Reference Guide to Medicinal Plants: Herbal Medicine Past and Present.* 2 volumes. Durham, N.C.: Duke University Press. 1990.

Dana, Mrs. William Starr. *How to Know the Wildflowers.* New York: Dover Books. 1963.

Densmore, Frances. *How Indians Use Wild Plants for Food, Medicine and Crafts.* 1928. Reprint edition. New York: Dover. 1974.

Duke, James A. "A Pointer Weed?" *Wild Foods Forum,* Volume 14, No. 1. Winter 2003.

Elliott, Doug. *Wild Roots: A Foragers Guide to the Edible and Medicinal Roots, Tubers, Corms and Rhizomes of North America.* Rochester, Vt.: Healing Arts Press. 1995.

Elpel, Thomas. *Botany in a Day.* Fourth edition. Pony, Mt.: HOPS Press. 2001.

Erichsen-Brown, Charlotte. *Medicinal and Other Uses of North American Plants: A Historical Survey with Special Reference to Eastern Indian Tribes.* New York: Dover. 1989.

Feltner, Harvey, M.D. *The Eclectic Materia Medica, Pharmacology, and Therapeutics.* 1927. Reprint edition. Portland, Or.: Eclectic Medical Publications. 1989.

Feltner, Harvey Wickes, and John Uri Lloyd. *King's American Dispensatory.* Eighteenth edition, third revision. 2 vols. 1898.

Reprint edition. Portland, Or.: Eclectic Medical Publications. 1983.

Ferguson, Mary and Richard M. Saunders. *Wildflowers through the Seasons*. New York: Arrowood Press. 1989.

Foster, Steven. *101 Medicinal Herbs*. Loveland, Co.: Interweave Press. 1998.

Foster, Steven and James A. Duke. *A Field Guide to Medicinal Plants and Herbs of Eastern and Central North America*. Second edition. New York: Houghton Mifflin Company. 2000.

Foster, Steven and Yue Chongxi. *Herbal Emissaries: Bringing Chinese Herbs to the West*. Rochester, Vt.: Healing Arts Press. 1992.

Gladstar, Rosemary and Pam Hirch, ed. *Planting the Future: Saving Our Medicinal Herbs*. Rochester, Vt.: Healing Arts Press. 2000.

Grieve, Mrs. M. *A Modern Herbal*, Volumes I and II. New York: Dover Books. 1971.

Griggs, Barbara. *Green Pharmacy*. Rochester, Vt.: Healing Arts Press. 1997.

Grossinger, Richard. *Planet Medicine*. Fifth edition. Berkeley, Ca.: North Atlantic Books. 1990.

Hamel, Paul B. and Mary U. Chiltoskey. *Cherokee Plants: Their Uses—A 400 Year History*. Published privately. 1975.

Harrington, H.D. and L.W. Durrell. *How to Identify Plants*. Athens, Oh.: Swallow Press. 1957. Reprinted, 1981.

Hemmerly, Thomas E. *Appalachian Wildflowers*. Athens, Ga.: University of Georgia Press. 2000.

Hoffmann, David. *The Complete Illustrated Holistic Herbal*. Rockport, Ma.: Element Books. 1996.

Hoffmann, David. *Therapeutic Herbalism: A Correspondence Course in Phytotherapy*. Privately published. 1994.

Houk, Rose. Eastern *Wildflowers: A Photographic Celebration from New England to the Heartland*. San Francisco: Chronicle Books. 1989.

Hudson, Tori. *Women's Encyclopedia of Natural Medicine: Alternative Therapies and Integrative Medicine.* Los Angeles, Ca.: Keats Publishing. 1999.

Hutchins, Alma. *Indian Herbalogy of North America.* Ninth edition. Ontario, Canada: Merco. 1983.

Hutson, Robert W., William F. Hutson and Aaron J. Sharp. *Great Smoky Mountain Wildflowers.* Northbrook, Il.: Windy Pines Publishing. 1962. Revised and expanded fifth edition. 1995.

Justice, William S. and C. Ritchie Bell. *Wildflowers of North Carolina.* Chapel Hill, N.C.: University of North Carolina Press. 1968.

Jones, Pamela. *Just Weeds: History, Myths and Uses.* Shelburne, Vt.: Chapters Publishing. 1994.

Kindscher, Kelly. *Medicinal Wild Plants of the Prairie.* Lawrence, Kansas: University Press of Kansas. 1992.

Krochmal, Arnold, Russell S. Waters and Richard M. Doughty. *A Guide to the Medicinal Plants of Appalachia.* Northeast Forest Experimental Station, Upper Darby, Pa.: USDA Forest Service Research Paper NE-138. 1969.

Kowalchik, Claire and William H. Hylton, ed. *Rodale's Illustrated Encyclopedia of Herbs.* Emmaus, Pa.: Rodale Press. 1987.

Kuhn, Merrily A. and David Winston. *Herbal Therapy and Supplements: A Scientific and Traditional Approach.* Philadelphia, Pa.: Lippincott Williams and Wilcox. 2000.

Kuriyama, Shigehisa. *The Expressiveness of the Body and Divergence of Greek and Chinese Medicine.* New York: Zone Books. 1999.

Libster, Martha. *Herbal Diplomats.* Lafayette, In.: Golden Apple Publications. 2004.

Lighthall, J. I. *The Indian Folk Medicine Guide.* New York: Popular Library. 1973.

Lust, John. *The Herb Book.* Simi Valley, Ca.: Benedict Lust Publications. 1974.

Bibliography

Martin, Laura C. *Wildflower Folklore*. Charlotte, N.C.: East Woods Press/Fast and McMillan Publishers. 1984.

Moerman, Daniel E. *Native American Ethnobotany*. Portland, Or.: Timber Press. 1998.

Mooney, James. "The Swimmer Manuscript: Cherokee Formulas and Medicinal Prescriptions." *Smithsonian Institution Bureau of American Ethnology, Bulletin 99*. Revised and edited by Frans M. Olbrechts. Washington, D.C.: United States Government Printing Office. 1932.

Moore, Michael. *Medicinal Plants of the Mountain West*. Santa Fe, N.M.: Museum of New Mexico Press. 1988.

Michael, Pamela and Christabell King. *All Good Things Around Us*. New York: Holt Rinehart Winston. 1980.

Newcomb, Lawrence. *Newcomb's Wildflower Guide*. Boston, Ma.: Little, Brown and Co. 1977.

Patton, Darryl. *Tommie Bass: Herb Doctor of Shinbone Ridge*. Birmingham, Al.: Back to Nature Publications. 1988.

Phillips, Harry R. *Growing and Propagating Wildflowers*. Chapel Hill, N.C.: University of North Carolina Press. 1985.

Porcher, Frances P. *Resources of the Southern Fields and Forests*. Charleston, Va.: Evans and Cogswell. 1863. Reprint edition. Arno Press. 1970.

Radford, Albert E., Harry E. Ahles and C. Ritchie Bell. *Manual of the Vascular Flora of the Carolinas*. Chapel Hill, N.C.: University of North Carolina Press. 1968.

Shook, Edward. *Advanced Treatise in Herbology*. 1946. Reprint edition. Beaumont, Ca.: Trinity Center Press. 1978.

Simoons, Frederick J. *Plants of Life, Plants of Death*. Madison, Wi.: The University of Wisconsin Press. 1998.

Smith, Richard M. *Wildflowers of the Southern Mountains*. Knoxville, Tn.: University of Tennessee Press. 1998.

Snow, Alice Micco and Susan Enns Stans. *Healing Plants:*

Medicine of the Florida Seminole Indians. Gainesville, Fl.: University Press of Florida. 2001.

Symonds, George W. D. *The Shrub Identification Book.* New York: William Morrow and Company. 1963.

Thoreau, Henry David. *The Heart of Thoreau's Journals.* Edited by Odell Shepard. New York: Dover Publications. 1961.

Timme, S. Lee. *Wildflowers of Mississippi.* Jackson, Ms.: University Press of Mississippi. 1989.

Winston, David. "Nvwote: Cherokee Medicine and Ethnobotany" *American Herbalism: Essays on Herbs and Herbalism* by the Members of the American Herbalists Guild. Michael Tierra, editor. Freedom, Ca.: Crossing Press. 1992.

Wigginton, Elliot, ed. *Foxfire 3.* Garden City, N.Y.: Anchor Press/Doubleday. 1975.

Wigginton, Elliot and Margie Bennett, ed. *Foxfire 9.* Garden City, N. Y.: Anchor Press/Doubleday. 1986.

Wofford, B. Eugene. *Guide to the Vascular Plants of the Blue Ridge.* Athens, Ga.: University of Georgia Press. 1989.

Wren, R.C. *Potter's New Cyclopaedia of Botanical Drugs and Preparations.* 1907. Revised edition. Essex, England: C. W. Daniel Company Limited. 1988.

Resources

Recommended Books

★ General Herb Books

The Complete Illustrated Holistic Herbal, David Hoffmann

Herbal Remedies for Dummies, Christopher Hobbs

Natural Healing with Herbs, Humbart Santillo

Rosemary Gladstar's Family Herbal, Rosemary Gladstar

★ Appalachian Plants

A Field Guide to Medicinal Plants and Herbs of Eastern and Central North America, Stephen Foster and James A. Duke

Appalachian Wildflowers, Thomas E. Hemmerly

Newcomb's Wildflower Guide, Lawrence Newcomb

Wildflowers of the Southern Mountains, Richard M. Smith

✷ Appalachian Folk Medicine

A Reference Guide to Medicinal Plants: Herbal Medicine Past and Present, James A. Crellin and Jane Philpott. (2 volumes.)

The Foxfire Book, Vol. 1-12, Elliot Wigginton, et. al, Editors

Folk Medicine of Southern Appalachia, Anthony Cavender

Tommie Bass: Herb Doctor of Shinbone Ridge, Darryl Patton

✷ Medicine Making

Handmade Herbal Medicines: Recipes for Potions, Elixirs and Salves, Christopher Hobbs

The Herbal Medicine Cabinet: Preparing Natural Remedies at Home, Debra St. Clair

The Medicine Maker's Handbook, James Green

Making Plant Medicines, Richo Chech

✷ Medicinal Herb Sites

Daniel Moerman's North American Ethnobotany Database
http://herb.umd.umich.edu
Native American Peoples use of plants.

Health World Materia Medica www.healthy.net
Searchable database of hundreds of herb monographs by David Hoffmann.

Henriette's Herbal Home Page www.henriettesherbal.com
Classic botanical texts, on-line forums and other useful information.

MedHerb www.medherb.com
An interactive electronic database that provides scientific data underlying the use of herbs for health.

Southwest School of Botanical Medicine www.swsbm.com
Herbalist Michael Moore's awe-inspiring website is like having an on-line herbal library at your fingertips. Classic botanical texts, photos, drawings, articles, downloadable books, and much more.

Sources of Herbs, Native Plants and Seeds

★ Herb Suppliers

Ethically harvested or organic sources of medicinal plants discussed in this book.

Bella Vita Botanicals 800-787-1615
www.bellavitabotanicals.com

Blessed Herbs 800-489-4372 www.blessedherbs.com

Frontier Natural Products Coop 800-669-3275
www.frontiercoop.com

GAIA Herbs 828-884-4242 www.gaiaherbs.com

Herbalist and Alchemist 800-611-8235
www.herbalist-alchemist.com

Moon Branch Botanicals 828-479-2788 www.moonbranch.com

Mountain Rose Herbs 800-879-3337
www.mountainroseherbs.com

Pacific Botanicals 541-479-7777 www.pacificbotanicals.com

✹ Native Plants

To find a local native plant nursery, check the Lady Bird Johnson Wildflower Directory. For mail order plants, contact individual suppliers.

National Directory of Native Plant Suppliers, Lady Bird Johnson Wildflower Center, Native Plant Information Network www.wildflower2.org/NPIN/suppliers/suppliers.html

Companion Plants 740-592-4643 http://companionplants.com

Niche Gardens 919-967-0078 www.nichegardens.com

Mail Order Natives 850-973-683 www.mailordernatives.com

North Carolina Ginseng and Goldenseal Co. 828-649-3536 www.ncgoldenseal.com

Sandy Mush Herb Nursery 828-683-2014 www.brwm.org/sandymushherbs

✹ Native Plant Seeds

Horizon Herbs 541-846-6704 www.horizonherbs.com

Johnny's Selected Seeds 207-861-3900 www.johnnyseeds.com

Richters Herbs 905-640-6677 www.richters.com

Southern Exposure 540-894-9480 www.southernexposure.com

Native Plant Information

★ Native Plant Societies

Native Plant Societies of the United States and Canada
Exhaustive list of native plant societies by state.
www.michbotclub.org/links/native_plant_society.htm

New England Wildflower Society
Formed in 1900 to promote the study and preservation of
wildflowers. www.newfs.org/hps.htm

Lady Bird Johnson Wildflower Center Largest wildflower
organization in the U.S. www.wildflower.org

Southern Appalachian Botanical Society
www.newberrynet.com/sabs/

★ Threatened and Endangered Plant Lists and Conservation Resources

Center for Plant Conservation Directory by State
www.centerforplantconservation.org/CPCDirectory/CPC_
DIR_find.asp

Federal Native Plant Conservation Committee
www.nps.gov/plants/coop.htm

**Plant Conservation Alliance – Medicinal Plants Working
Group** www.nps.gov/plants/medicinal/index.htm

Southeast Rare Plant Information Network (SERPIN)
www.serpin.org/index1.html

Threatened and Endangered Species: SE Region
www.fws.gov/southeast/es/T2E%20species.htm

US Fish and Wildlife Service – Species Information:
Threatened and Endangered Plants
www.fws.gov/endangered/wildlife.html

United Plant Savers 802-479-9823 www.unitedplantsavers.org

Bloom and Harvest Calendars

Bloom Calendar

Common Name	Jan	Feb	Mar	Apr	May	Jun	Jul	Aug	Sep	Oct	Nov	Dec
Bethroot				■	■							
Black Cohosh						■	■					
Black Haw					■	■						
Black Walnut				■	■							
Bloodroot			■	■								
Blue Cohosh				■	■							
Boneset								■	■	■		
Devil's Walking Stick						■	■					
Dogwood					■	■						
Elder						■	■					
Evening Primrose								■	■			
Fringetree					■	■						
Gentian									■	■		
Ginseng, American						■	■					
Goldenrod								■	■	■		
Indian Pipe							■	■				
Jewelweed								■	■	■		
Joe-pye-weed							■	■	■	■		
Lobelia								■	■	■		
Maidenhair Fern	No Flowers											
Mountain Mint						■	■	■				
Partridgeberry						■	■					
Passionflower							■	■				

Bloom Calendar

Common Name	Jan	Feb	Mar	Apr	May	Jun	Jul	Aug	Sep	Oct	Nov	Dec
Pipsissewa						▓	▓	▓				
Pleurisy Root							▓	▓	▓			
Rabbit Tobacco								▓	▓	▓		
Red Root						▓	▓	▓				
Sarsaparilla						▓	▓					
Sassafras				▓	▓				▓			
Skullcap						▓	▓	▓				
Solomon's Seal					▓	▓						
Spicebush			▓	▓								
Stoneroot							▓	▓				
Sumac						▓	▓	▓				
Sweet Gum				▓	▓							
Sweetfern						▓	▓					
Turtlehead								▓	▓			
Virginia Snakeroot					▓	▓	▓					
Wild Cherry				▓	▓							
Wild Geranium				▓	▓	▓						
Wild Ginger				▓	▓							
Wild Hydrangea						▓	▓					
Wild Yam						▓	▓					
Witch Hazel									▓	▓	▓	▓
Yellowroot							▓	▓				

Common Name	Part Used	Jan	Feb	Mar	Apr	May	Jun	Jul	Aug	Sep	Oct	Nov	Dec
Bethroot	root								■	■			
Black Cohosh	root									■	■		
Black Haw	bark		■	■	■								
Black Walnut	leaf, hull					Leaf				Hull			
Bloodroot	root									■	■		
Blue Cohosh	root									■	■		
Boneset	aerial (in flower)								■	■			
Devil's Walking Stick	berry, bark	■			Bark					Berry		Bark	
Dogwood	bark (aged one year)	■	■									Bark	■
Elder	flower, leaf, berry (bark)			Bark		Leaf	Flower		Berry			Bark	
Evening Primrose	entire plant						■	■					
Fringetree	dried root bark			■	■								
Gentian	root									■	■		
Ginseng, American	root, leaf					Leaf				Root			
Goldenrod	aerial (in flower)								■	■			
Indian Pipe	entire plant						■	■					
Jewelweed	aerial (before flower fades)						■	■					
Joe-pye-weed	leaf or root							Leaf			Root		
Lobelia	aerial (in flower)								■	■			
Maidenhair Fern	fronds, root						■	■	■				
Mountain Mint	aerial (in flower)							■	■				
Partridgeberry	aerial										■	■	■
Passionflower	leaf and flower						■	■	■				

Common Name	Part Used	Jan	Feb	Mar	Apr	May	Jun	Jul	Aug	Sep	Oct	Nov	Dec
Pipsissewa	leaf	▓	▓					▓	▓	▓	▓	▓	▓
Pleurisy Root	root									▓	▓		
Rabbit Tobacco	aerial (in flower)												
Red Root	root, leaf					Root			Leaf		Root		
Sarsaparilla	root												
Sassafras	root bark, bark, leaf		Root bark			Bark			Leaf	▓			
Skullcap	aerial (in flower)						▓	▓	▓	▓			
Solomon's Seal	root												
Spicebush	leaf, bark, twig, berry			Leaf, Bark, Twig						Berry			
Stoneroot	entire plant (in flower)						Leaf						
Sumac	berry, leaf						Leaf				Berry		
Sweet Gum	resin (gum), leaf, inner bark			Bark	Resin		Leaf						
Sweetfern	leaf						▓						
Turtlehead	aerial (in flower)									▓	▓		
Virginia Snakeroot	root												
Wild Cherry	bark, fruit							Fruit			Bark		
Wild Geranium	root, leaf						Leaf	Root					
Wild Ginger	root										▓		
Wild Hydrangea	root bark										▓		▓
Wild Yam	root												
Witch Hazel	leaf, bark				▓		▓						
Yellow Root	root												

229

THERAPEUTIC INDEX

This index is provided as a quick, general guide for finding the right herb to treat a specific symptom or condition. Once you find an herb or several herbs that address the symptoms you are treating, look up each in Chapter 3 to determine if its specific actions will be effective and to find out how to use it correctly. Below, an underlined herb indicates a specific remedy for the symptoms or condition. You may want to start your research by looking up these herbs first.

You can begin your herbal treatment in one of two ways: by using one herb to see what its effect will be, or by creating a simple formula that combines several herbs that have complimentary actions.

For example, when treating a cold you may need to reduce a fever, soothe a sore throat and help promote sleep. To do this you may find one herb that combines all three actions, or you may need to use two or more herbs that together address all the symptoms. The art of herbal formulation is beyond the scope of this book, but you can begin to teach yourself about herbal therapies by choosing to use several herbs together in a simple formula. It is always best to start out with only one to three herbs and use them for a day or two before deciding that they do or don't work for you. If they don't have the desired effect, try another herb or herbs. And always be certain that your herbs are of the highest quality.

Abscess
Elder leaf, evening primrose (external), red root (internal)

Acne
Sweetfern (external)

Allergies (Seasonal/Hay Fever)
Elderberry, elder flower, <u>goldenrod</u>, lobelia

Amenorrhea
Partridgeberry

Anemia
<u>Ginseng</u>, rabbit tobacco, wild cherry

Appetite loss
Boneset, <u>gentian</u>, ginseng, turtlehead, Virginia snakeroot, wild cherry

Anal Fistula
Red root (internal)

Anxiety
Black cohosh, evening primrose, ginseng, <u>passionflower</u>, <u>skullcap</u>, wild cherry

Arthritis (see also Joint pain/stiffness)
<u>Black cohosh</u>, black haw, devil's walking stick, wild yam

Asthma (Acute symptoms)
Black haw, bloodroot, blue cohosh, <u>lobelia</u>, rabbit tobacco

Bladder Infections
Goldenrod, Joe-pye-weed, <u>pipsissewa</u>, wild cherry, wild hydrangea, wild yam

Bleeding (Wounds)
Sweetfern, sumac, <u>wild geranium</u>

Bleeding (Internal)
Wild geranium

Blood Pressure (High)
Ginseng, passionflower

Boils
Elder leaf, evening primrose

Breast Lumps/Cysts (Fibrocystic Breast Disease)
Red root

Breast Pain (Fibrocystic Breast Disease)
Red root

Bronchitis
Black cohosh, bloodroot, blue cohosh, boneset, evening primrose, sarsaparilla, wild cherry

Burns
Elder leaf, goldenrod, red root, sumac, sweetfern, witch hazel

Breathing Difficulties
Goldenrod, lobelia

Bruises (External)
Elder leaf, fringetree, Solomon's seal, witch hazel

Cancer
Bloodroot (external), red root (internal)

Canker Sores
Red root, wild geranium, yellowroot

Cold Sores
Red root, wild geranium, yellowroot

Congestion, Lung (see also Cold, Cough, Influenza, and Sinusitis)
Bloodroot, <u>boneset</u>, <u>elderberry</u>, <u>elder flower</u>, goldenrod, maidenhair fern, pleurisy root, rabbit tobacco, sassafras, spicebush, sweet gum, wild cherry

Circulation
<u>Red root</u>, Virginia snakeroot, wild ginger

Colds
<u>Boneset</u>, <u>elderberry</u>, elder flower, goldenrod, Joe-pye-weed, rabbit tobacco, sassafras, spicebush, sumac, sweet gum, wild cherry

Conjunctivitis
Wild cherry, wild geranium, <u>yellowroot</u>

Constipation
Black walnut, boneset, elderberry, <u>gentian</u>, yellowroot

Cough
Bethroot, <u>black cohosh</u>, bloodroot, blue cohosh, <u>elderberry</u>, elder flower, evening primrose, ginseng, maidenhair fern, pleurisy root, rabbit tobacco, sarsaparilla, Solomon's seal, sumac, <u>wild cherry</u>, wild ginger

Cramp (see also Menstrual Cramps)
<u>Black haw</u>, lobelia, passionflower, skullcap, wild yam

Cystitis
Joe-pye-weed, <u>goldenrod</u>, wild hydrangea, wild yam

Debility
Gentian, ginseng

Decongestant (See Congestion, Lung)

Depression
Black cohosh (post-partum), <u>gentian</u>, ginseng

Diarrhea
Dogwood, <u>goldenrod</u>, sumac, sweet gum, sweetfern, <u>wild geranium</u>, witch hazel

Diverticulitis
Black haw, wild yam

Drug/Alcohol Withdrawal
Skullcap

Earache
Devil's walking stick

Eczema
Bloodroot, evening primrose, jewelweed, red root (internal), sassafras (internal)

Endometriosis
Black cohosh, blue cohosh, Indian pipe (pain), <u>partridgeberry</u>, red root

Eye Irritation (External)
Evening primrose, wild cherry, witch hazel

Fatigue
<u>Gentian</u>, <u>ginseng</u>, sarsaparilla, skullcap, Solomon's seal, wild cherry

Fever
<u>Boneset,</u> dogwood, elderberry, <u>elder flower</u>, Joe-pye-weed, mountain mint, sassafras, spice bush, sweet gum, sumac, wild cherry, wild ginger

Flatulence (Gas)
Bloodroot, <u>mountain mint</u>, sassafras, spice bush, sweetfern

Fibrocystic Breast Disease
Red root

Fibromyalgia
Black cohosh, partridgeberry, <u>passionflower, skullcap</u>

Fungal Infection/Growths
<u>Black walnut</u>, bloodroot, yellowroot

Gallbladder Inflammation/Stones
<u>Fringetree</u>, stoneroot, turtlehead

Gas (see Flatulence)

Gastritis
Wild cherry, wild geranium, <u>wild yam</u>, yellowroot

Gingivitis
<u>Bloodroot</u>, sumac, sweetfern, yellowroot

Glands (Swollen)
Pleurisy root, <u>red root</u>

Gout
Indian pipe (acute), <u>sassafras</u>, wild yam (acute)

Headache
Black cohosh, gentian, passionflower, skullcap

Hemorrhoids
Stoneroot, wild geranium, <u>witch hazel</u>

Heartburn
<u>Gentian</u>, goldenrod, mountain mint, yellowroot

Hay Fever (see Allergies)

Hoarseness (see Laryngitis)

Immune Stimulant
<u>Boneset, elderberry</u>, elder flower, ginseng, sarsaparilla

Incontinence
Pipsissewa

Indigestion
Bloodroot, boneset, <u>gentian</u>, ginseng, goldenrod, mountain mint, sassafras, <u>turtlehead</u>, wild cherry, yellowroot

Infection
See also Bladder Infection, Respiratory Infection, Skin Infection, Viral Infection

Infertility
Partridgeberry

Influenza
<u>Boneset,</u> <u>elderberry</u>, elder flower, goldenrod, Joe-pye-weed, sassafras

Insect Bites
Elder leaf, evening primrose, goldenrod, <u>jewelweed</u>, wild geranium, <u>witch hazel</u>

Insomnia
Black cohosh, ginseng, <u>passionflower</u>, <u>skullcap</u>, wild cherry

Interstitial Cystitis
<u>Goldenrod</u>, Joe-pye-weed, pipsissewa

Irritable Bowel Syndrome
<u>Black haw</u>, passionflower, sassafras, sweet gum, wild cherry, <u>wild yam</u>

Itching
Elder leaf, evening primrose, <u>jewelweed</u>, sumac, sweetfern

Jaundice
Bloodroot, <u>fringetree</u>, redroot, turtlehead

Joint Pain/Stiffness
Devil's walking stick, ginseng, Joe-pye-weed, passionflower

Kidney Stones
Goldenrod, Joe-pye-weed, stoneroot, wild hydrangea

Kidney Tonic
Joe-pye-weed, pipsissewa, wild hydrangea

Labor Tonics/Aids
Black cohosh, black haw, blue cohosh, partridgeberry

Laryngitis
Elder flower, goldenrod, maidenhair fern, wild cherry

Leucorrhea (see also Vaginitis)
Black walnut, partridgeberry, red root, sumac, sweetfern, wild geranium

Liver Tonics (Hepatic)
Fringetree, red root, turtlehead

Lung Congestion (see Congestion, Lung)

Menopause
Black cohosh, black haw, blue cohosh, partridgeberry, skullcap, wild yam

Menstruation (Delayed)
Blue cohosh, partridgeberry, spicebush

Menstruation (Excessive)
Bethroot, black haw, partridgeberry, sweet gum, wild geranium

Menstruation (Cramps/Pain)
Black cohosh, black haw, Indian pipe, partridgeberry, passion-flower, red root, skullcap, spicebush, wild yam

Migraine
Passionflower, lobelia, gentian, <u>skullcap</u>

Miscarriage (Threatened)
Black haw, blue cohosh, partridgeberry

Morning Sickness
Mountain mint, wild ginger, <u>wild yam</u>

Motion Sickness
Mountain mint, wild ginger

Mouth ulcers (see also Canker Sores, Cold Sores)
Bloodroot, red root, sumac, wild geranium, <u>yellowroot</u>

Muscle Stiffness/Sprains
<u>Black haw</u>, ginseng, lobelia, passionflower, skullcap, <u>wild yam</u>, witch hazel

Nausea
<u>Mountain mint</u>, sassafras, sweet gum, sweetfern, <u>wild ginger</u>, wild yam

Nicotine (Cigarette) **Withdrawal**
Skullcap

Ovarian pain
Black haw, <u>blue cohosh</u>, Indian pipe

Pain
Boneset, devil's walking stick, <u>Indian pipe</u>, Joe-pye-weed, skullcap, wild ginger, wild hydrangea, wild yam, witch hazel

Palpitations (Heart)
Black cohosh, black haw, passionflower, wild yam

Pertussis (see Whooping Cough)

Peptic Ulcers
Yellowroot

Poison Ivy Rash
Elder leaf, jewelweed, sassafras, sweetfern

Pre-Menstrual Syndrome (PMS)
<u>Black cohosh</u>, blue cohosh, black haw, partridgeberry, <u>passion-flower</u>, skullcap, wild yam

Pregnancy (Fertility Tonics)
Blue cohosh, partridge berry

Pregnancy (Morning Sickness)
Mountain mint, wild ginger, <u>wild yam</u>

Pregnancy (Threatened Miscarriage)
Black haw, blue cohosh, partridgeberry

Psoriasis
Elder leaf, evening primrose, jewelweed, red root (internal), sassafras (internal)

Prostatitis
Joe-pye-weed, pipsissewa, stoneroot, wild hydrangea

Pulmonary Edema
Pleurisy root

Reproductive System Tonic (Female)
Partridgeberry

Respiratory Infections (see also Congestion, Lung, Cough, Decongestants, Viral Infections)
<u>Boneset,</u> <u>elderberry</u>, pleurisy root, sarsaparilla, Solomon's seal, spicebush, stoneroot, sweet gum

Rheumatism
<u>Black cohosh</u>, black haw, boneset, <u>devil's walking stick</u>, Joe-pye-weed, sassafras, wild yam

Sciatica
Black haw, skullcap

Skin Rash
<u>Elder leaf</u>, evening primrose, <u>jewelweed</u>, red root, sumac, sweet gum, sweetfern, wild cherry, wild geranium

Skin Infection
Bloodroot, elder leaf, evening primrose, jewelweed, wild geranium, <u>yellowroot</u>

Sinusitis
Elderberry, <u>elder flower</u>, <u>goldenrod</u>, mountain mint, yellowroot

Sore Throat
Evening primrose, goldenrod, maidenhair fern, sumac, <u>sweet gum</u>, sweetfern, wild cherry, wild ginger, witch hazel, <u>yellowroot</u>

Stress/Tension
Evening primrose, ginseng, passionflower, sarsaparilla, skullcap, rabbit tobacco, wild cherry

Tinnitus
Black cohosh

Toothache
<u>Devil's walking stick</u>, Indian pipe

Uterine Fibroids
Blue cohosh

Uterine Pain
Black cohosh

Vaginitis/Vaginal Discharge/Infection (External)
<u>Black walnut</u>, partridgeberry, sumac, sweetfern, <u>wild geranium</u>

Varicose veins
Stoneroot, witch hazel (external)

Vascular Tonic
Stoneroot

Viral Infections (see also Influenza)
Boneset, elderberry

Vomiting
Mountain mint, sassafras, wild ginger

Warts
Bloodroot (external)

Whooping cough (see also Coughs, Decongestants)
<u>Black cohosh</u>, black haw, bloodroot, pleurisy root, Virginia
snakeroot, wild cherry

Worms/Parasites
Black walnut

Wounds
Bloodroot, <u>elder leaf</u>, evening primrose, fringetree, goldenrod,
jewelweed, sumac, <u>sweet gum</u>, <u>yellowroot</u>

Yeast Infections (Candidiasis)
Black walnut

Index

245

Index

Index

251

Index

Index

About the Author

Patricia Kyritsi Howell is the owner of BotanoLogos, a school that provides experiential learning about edible and medicinal plants of the Southern Appalachians. Since 1991, she has introduced herbalism to thousands of students, in the United States and Europe, always emphasizing first-hand knowledge of the plants themselves. Patricia is a Registered Herbalist and has been a professional member of the American Herbalists Guild since 1995. She is co-owner of a travel company: Wild Crete, which offers tours to explore herbs, wildflowers and traditional cuisines on the Greek island of Crete.

Learn More

Learn More about the Medicinal Plants of the Southern Appalachians...

. . .at BotanoLogos,* a school in the northeast Georgia mountains dedicated to awakening students' innate abilities to use medicinal and edible plants for healing and other forms of nourishment. Programs emphasize the use of wild, native, medicinal herbs that have been used traditionally in the Southern Appalachian Mountains. Students learn historical and current uses as well as practical, up-to-date information about a wide range of other plants that grow in the region.

Classroom and outdoor program offerings include: an annual Herbal Studies Certification Program; seasonal plant walks; workshops about field botany, ethical harvesting, and hands-on medicine making; seminars about herbal therapeutics and the practice of herbalism; and variations of these topics in delightful programs for children of every age.

BotanoLogos is located in the northeast Georgia mountains in Rabun County (100 miles northeast of midtown Atlanta, Georgia, and 90 miles southwest of Asheville, NC).

For more information, or to be included on our mailing list, you may visit www.botanologos.com or phone 706-746-5485.

*Botanologos is an ancient Greek word that means, "someone who speaks for the plants."

To Order More Copies

To Order More Copies of
Medicinal Plants of the Southern Appalachians
by Patricia Kyritsi Howell

For each book, you may send a check or money order, made payable to BotanoLogos Books, in the amount of $19.95, plus $3.00 per book for postage and handling (Georgia residents please add 7% sales tax).

Mailing address:
BotanoLogos Books
PO Office Box W,
Mountain City, Georgia 30562-0917.

To place a phone order, call 706-746-5485 and have your Visa or MasterCard ready. Discount rates are available for orders of 10 or more books; please enquire. Or, visit your local independent bookstore.

LaVergne, TN USA
01 November 2009
162665LV00003BA/4/A